ROBERT LOWELL

Burton Raffel

FREDERICK UNGAR PUBLISHING CO.
NEW YORK

Library of Congress Cataloging in Publication Data

Raffel, Burton.
   Robert Lowell.

   (Modern literature series)
   Bibliography: p.
   Includes index.
   1. Lowell, Robert, 1917–1977—Criticism and interpreta-
tion.   I. Title.   II. Series.
PS3523.089Z84   811'.52   81-40470
ISBN 0-8044-2707-0   AACR2

for Michael London—

*who fourteen years ago asked me to write
an essay on Lowell, and after reading (and
rejecting) the essay, said: "Burton, write a book."*

Acknowledgment is gratefully made as follows for permission to reprint copyrighted material:

From LIFE STUDIES by Robert Lowell. Copyright © 1956, 1959 by Robert Lowell. From FOR THE UNION DEAD by Robert Lowell. Copyright © 1956, 1960, 1961, 1962, 1963, 1964 by Robert Lowell. From NEAR THE OCEAN by Robert Lowell. Copyright © 1963, 1965, 1966, 1967 by Robert Lowell. From NOTEBOOK 1967–1968 by Robert Lowell. Copyright © 1967, 1968, 1969 by Robert Lowell. From THE DOLPHIN by Robert Lowell. Copyright © 1973 by Robert Lowell. From DAY BY DAY by Robert Lowell. Copyright © 1973, 1976, 1977 by Robert Lowell. From IMITATIONS by Robert Lowell. Copyright © 1958, 1959, 1960, 1961 by Robert Lowell. From PHAEDRA by Robert Lowell. Copyright © 1960, 1961 by Robert Lowell. From THE OLD GLORY by Robert Lowell. Copyright © 1964, 1965, 1968 by Robert Lowell. From THE ORESTIA by Robert Lowell. Copyright © 1978 by Robert Silvers and State Street Bank and Trust Company, Executors of the Estate of Robert Lowell.

For passages from R. C. Knight's translation of Racine's *Phèdre* by courtesy of Edinburgh University Press.

SELECTED POEMS of Eugenio Montale, translated by Irma Brandeis. Copyright © 1965 by New Directions Publishing Corportion. Reprinted by permission of New Directions.

Ezra Pound, PERSONAE. Copyright 1926 by Ezra Pound. Reprinted by permission of New Directions.

Passages from George Dillon's translation of Racine's *Phèdre* from *Three Plays of Racine*, © 1961 by the University of Chicago, and for Richmond Lattimore's translation of Aeschylus' *Agamemnon* from *Complete Greek Tragedies*. Copyright, 1942, by the University of Chicago, by courtesy of University of Chicago Press.

For selections from Kate Flores's translation of Leopardi's *L'Infinito* from Leopardi, *Poems and Prose* edited by Angel Flores by courtesy of Indiana University Press. Copyright © 1966 by Indiana University Press.

From "Saratoga Ending" by Welden Kees reprinted from *Collected Poems* by Weldon Kees by permission of University of Nebraska Press. Copyright © 1943, 1947, 1954 by Weldon Kees, Copyright © 1960 by John A. Kees.

From Boris Pasternak, *In the Wood* from *the Penguin Book of Russian Verse*, ed. Dimitri Obolensky (The Penguin Poets, Revised edition, 1965), p. 332. Copyright © Dimitri Obolensky, 1962, 1965, reprinted by permission of Penguin Books Ltd.

Lines from "Sunday Morning" by Wallace Stevens from *Collected Poems of Wallace Stevens*. Copyright 1923, etc., by Wallace Stevens, and lines from *Phèdre* translated by R. Henderson in *Six Plays by Corneille and Racine*. Copyright, 1931, by The Modern Library, by courtesy of Alfred A. Knopf, Inc., and Random House.

Contents

Chronology

1917   Robert Traill Spence Lowell, Jr. is born in Boston on 1 March.

1924–1930   He attends Brimmer School, in Boston.

1930–1935   He attends St. Mark's School, Southborough, Mass.

1935–1937   He studies at Harvard. In late spring and summer, he spends three months with Allen Tate and Caroline Gordon, Mrs. Tate, at their home in Clarksville, Tennessee, living in a tent on the Tates' lawn. (Ford Madox Ford and entourage were already installed as houseguests.)

1937–1940   He studies at Kenyon College, Gambier, Ohio, graduating summa cum laude with a classics major and studying with John Crowe Ransom. His friends include fellow students Randall Jarrell and Peter Taylor. He becomes a Roman Catholic and on April 2, 1940, marries the novelist Jean Stafford.

1940–1941   He teaches English at Kenyon and takes graduate courses in English at Lousiana State University, studying with Cleanth Brooks and Robert Penn Warren.

1941–1942   He works at Sheed & Ward, Roman Catholic publishing house in New York City, as an editorial assistant.

1942–1943   He lives with the Tates for a second time and works at *Land of Unlikeness*. Refusing to serve in the armed forces, he is tried, convicted, and sentenced to a year and a day in the federal prison at Danbury, Connecticut; he is paroled roughly halfway through his sentence.

1944   *Land of Unlikeness* is published in July, by the Cummington Press, a small publisher of literary books. After a brief residence in Maine, Lowell moves to New York City.

1946   *Lord Weary's Castle* is published by a major trade publisher, Harcourt, Brace, and wins the Pulitzer Prize.

1947   He wins a Guggenheim Fellowship and the American Academy of Arts and Letters Prize and serves as Poetry Consultant to the Library of Congress, Washington, D.C.

1948   In June he is divorced from Jean Stafford.

1949   He serves on the prize committee for the first Bollingen Prize, which is awarded to Ezra Pound for the *Pisan Cantos*. On July 28 he marries Elizabeth Hardwick.

1950   The British publisher, Faber and Faber, brings out *Poems 1938–49*. He teaches at the University of Iowa and at Kenyon. His father dies.

1950–1953   He lives and travels in Europe.

1951   *The Mills of the Kavanaughs* is published.

1953–1954   He teaches at Iowa, along with John Berryman; among his students is W. D. Snodgrass. He teaches at the University of Indiana and at the University of Cincinnati. His mother dies in February, 1954.

1954–1960   He lives in Boston, for the last five years teaching at Boston University; among his students were Anne Sexton, Sylvia Plath, and George Starbuck.

1957   His daughter, Harriet Winslow, is born.

1959   *Life Studies* is published and wins the National Book Award.

1960   He receives a Ford Foundation award for study of the opera.

1960–1970   He lives in New York City.

1961   *Imitations* is published and is co-winner of the Bollingen Translation Prize. His version of Racine's *Phaedra* is published.

1963–1967   He teaches at Harvard

1964   *For the Union Dead* is published; two of the three plays published as *The Old Glory* are produced at the American Place Theatre, in New York City, and one of the plays, "Benito Cereno," wins the Obie award for the best off-Broadway play.

1965   He first agrees to participate, then publicly declines, in a letter to President Lyndon B. Johnson, to attend the White House Festival of the Arts, as a protest against the Vietnam War.

1967   *Near the Ocean* is published. He serves as writer-in-residence at the Yale School of Drama, where his *Prometheus Bound* is performed.

1968   A revised edition of *The Old Glory* is published.

1969   *Notebook 1967–68* and *Prometheus Bound* are published.

1970   *Notebook* is published. Lowell is named a Visiting Fellow at All Souls College, Oxford.

1970–1976   He lives in England; from 1970–1972 he teaches at Essex University.

1971   His son, Robert Sheridan, is born; the child's mother is Caroline Blackwood.

1972   He is divorced from Elizabeth Hardwick and, in October, is married to Caroline Blackwood.

1973   *The Dolphin, History,* and *For Lizzie and Harriet* are published, and *The Dolphin* wins the Pulitzer Prize.

1976   Faber and Faber publishes *Selected Poems*.

1977   *Day by Day* is published. He returns to the United States and to Elizabeth Hardwick. On September 12 he dies, in New York City, at the age of sixty.

1

From Boston to New York: A Sketch of Life and Work

Robert Lowell will never be a "popular" poet—and he would have been chagrined, probably even pained, to know that basic and obviously unpleasant truth. He was not an easy poet, someone who, like Rod McKuen, leaves out anything and everything disturbing, someone who panders to contemporary taste while indulging himself (and his readers) in perpetual sentimentalizations. Poets like McKuen are carried smoothly, effortlessly along on a wide current of uplifting goodwill; poets like Robert Lowell find it impossible not to struggle with—rather than corrupt or ignore—reality. On the other hand, there are also poets like William Wordsworth, and John Milton, and Robert Browning, and William Shakespeare, who achieve and maintain a kind of abiding popularity, though they are no more facile, no more mindless (to say the least) than was Robert Lowell.

For though Lowell is without question a poet of large talents, and also of large achievement, though he was much honored and reasonably widely read during his lifetime, and will never be forgotten now that he is dead, though some called him a great poet and almost no one was ever able to ignore him, or ever will be able to ignore him, he was from the start impossible to classify in any simple way. And as he moved through the stages

of a forty-year career, he changed more than most men,
or most poets, are likely to change. Lowell's life, like his
career, swung between poles separated by immense
distance, and that too is typical of the man and of the
poet. He can be viewed—as I myself view him—as a
great poet who for the most part refused to write great
poetry. He can be viewed—as others have seen him—
as unquestionably the leading poet of his generation,
the moulder and maker of forms and approaches followed
and depended upon by a host of lesser writers. Or he
may be viewed as a poet thrust into prominence, un-
justifiably on the whole, by critics and publicists in
search of "greatness" to write about.

Certainly, he had a major effect on the literary
scene both in the United States and in England. The
large and important group of poets known, loosely and
somewhat inaccurately, as the confessional school—poets
who wring their autobiographies and their tears and
their sins into their poems—is without question derived
more from Lowell than from any other poet, living or
dead. The group includes, just to indicate something of
Lowell's impact, such poets as Sylvia Plath, Ann Sexton,
and W.D. Snodgrass, all of them winners of major prizes
and much critical praise. But it is also worth noting that
all three, for all their successes and their fame, have led
basically unstable and unhappy lives. Snodgrass's first
and best book, *Heart's Needle,* stems largely from the
incidents and the feelings surrounding his divorce and
the separation it involved from his dearly loved small
daughter. And both Sexton and Plath, the latter quite
young, the former in middle life, committed suicide.
Lowell himself was in and out of mental institutions
much of his life; none of his three marriages endured,
and at his death he had just left his third wife and was
again living with his second.

Born to Protestantism, he had early converted to
Catholicism, then left that faith—just as, after his second

divorce, he left the United States and went to live in England with his third wife, not only a British aristocrat but a titled one.

In some basic ways, I think, Lowell was a man looking for a center, a steady core, which as both man and poet he never found. The prose autobiography printed as the second and longest portion of his best book, *Life Studies*, makes clear that Lowell's childhood (he was an only child) was deeply unhappy, plagued by a powerful, demanding, manipulative mother and an ambitious but weak and bungling father. He speaks of his mother as "hysterical even in her calm," and of his father's "submissive tenacity." He also speaks of the "atmosphere of glacial purity and sacrifice" in which this tormented and tormenting family dwelled. "Oh Bobby, it's such a comfort to have a man in the house," he records his mother as exclaiming, one Christmas Eve when his father was unable to be at home. "I am not a man," Lowell records himself as replying, "I am a boy." No wonder that, in a poem in this same book, he describes his mother's coffin, returning from abroad, as "wrapped like *panetone* [a large Milanese cake] in Italian tinfoil"—or that in a memorial poem to his father he describes him as "inattentive and beaming" and in yet another memorial poem as "cheerful and cowed." Stability and even sanity are hard to come by, when one grows from such roots.

But Robert Lowell's roots are vastly more complex and interesting than his quarrelsome and inept parents. There is an old doggerel saying about the New England (and specifically the Boston) aristocracy from which he comes: "And this is good old Boston,/ The home of the bean and the cod,/ Where the Lowells talk to the Cabots/ And the Cabots talk only to God." Lowell's ancestors include clergymen, congressmen, generals, judges, and perhaps most interesting of all, poets—most particularly James Russell Lowell (1819–1891), an internationally famous writer and critic, and Amy Lowell (1874–1925), perhaps equally famous as a poet associated with Ezra Pound and Hilda Doolittle (H.D.) and others in the Imagist movement early in this century, and as a cigar-smoking woman of great bulk and flagrant unconventionality. James Russell Lowell's older brother, Robert Traill Spence (1816–1891)—for whom Robert Lowell was named; his full name is Robert Traill Spence Lowell, Jr.—was a clergyman and novelist, as well as a minor poet. James Russell Lowell's first wife, Maria White (1821–1853), was a reasonably well-known poet in her own right. Abbott Lawrence Lowell, Amy's older brother, was president of Harvard University from 1909 to 1933. And James Russell Lowell was, finally, Robert Lowell's paternal great-granduncle. The Winslow side of his heredity includes no such literary forebears, but a long line of aristocrats and civic leaders, running back to Josiah Winslow, governor of Plymouth Colony, and Edward Winslow, who arrived on the Mayflower and was also a governor of Plymouth Colony.

This long and somewhat daunting heritage was plainly of immense importance to Lowell, sometimes as a foil against which to struggle, sometimes as a support upon which to lean. Not properly speaking a "rebel," at least in the usual senses of the word, there was nevertheless a continual turmoil and violence in Lowell. His lifelong nickname, for example, was "Cal," and he earned it early in life because his behavior reminded his friends and schoolmates of the violent and extravagant Roman Emperor, Caligula. He went to excellent and exclusive private schools, though his parents were said always to be short of funds and bickering about this as well as most other issues. At St. Mark's, where he boarded for six years, he began to write poetry, under the guidance— for better and for worse—of one of the most academic of twentieth-century American poets, Richard Eberhart. Eberhart gave him encouragement and sympathy, which he needed, and a taste for the melodramatic, the ornate, and the formal, which he did not. Eberhart's judgment of the adolescent poet was that he had a "heavy" mind and a disposition "essentially religious." The characterizations seem to me to tell us quite as much about the teacher as about the pupil.

Lowell moved on to Harvard in 1935, aged eighteen, but lasted only two years. He seems to have done very little work, to have drunk much and smoked up a lot, and to have pursued and conquered a girl some half a dozen years older than himself—in a quarrel with his father, over this young lady, he hit and knocked down the older man. He did not like Harvard, and Harvard did not much like him. Robert Frost, visiting the university, found the young man's early poetry long-winded and boring, as indeed it was. Lowell was introduced to, and tried to imitate, the work of William Carlos Williams, an experimenter in free language and forms. Lowell's imitative experiments did not work. Reeling from one pole to another, Lowell was urged by two new literary mentors, the British writer Ford Madox Ford and Dr. Merrill Moore—who was also the psychiatrist his parents had sent him to—to look up Allen Tate, a leader of the group of Southern writers known as the Fugitives. Fearfully literary himself, Tate was cordial and even flattered when the young Lowell showed up, uninvited, at his Tennessee home. Lowell was enthralled and asked if he could stay. Tate had other guests and no room. "You'd have to camp out on the lawn, in a tent," he is supposed to have said—and the earnest, confused Lowell rushed to a sporting goods store, bought a tent, and in fact camped out on Tate's lawn, in a tent, for the rest of the summer of 1937, imbibing daily infusions of Tate's theories and Tate's own poetic practice, both of which emphasized formal, highly rhetorical lines in regular meters and conventional structures. Tate had not yet converted to Catholicism, but he was deeply Christian; Tate's wife, Caroline Gordon, a well-known novelist, was Catholic. And so too was the young writer, Jean Stafford, whom Lowell met for the first time in 1937 and married in 1940, shortly after his own conversion to Catholicism.

In the autumn of 1937, strengthened by Tate's flattering attentions, Lowell transferred to Kenyon College, in Gambier, Ohio, where he studied with yet another Fugitive poet, John Crowe Ransom, and met, among others, the poet Randall Jarrell, three years Lowell's senior and, like Lowell, struggling to define himself as a writer. Neither Kenyon nor Ransom proved deeply stimulating, but Lowell read widely, studied classical and English literature, and finally graduated in 1940. He taught at Kenyon, took graduate courses in English literature at Louisiana State University—where he studied under two more of the South's leading figures, the novelist and poet Robert Penn Warren and the critic Cleanth Brooks—and came to New York, to work briefly as an editorial assistant at a Catholic publishing house. He had already determined that World War Two was a foolish mistake, playing into the hands of the Communists. The next year he wrote directly to President Franklin Roosevelt, explaining that "I cannot participate in this war, not because I think wars are contrary to my religion, but because I believe that the conduct of this war is a betrayal of my country." Toward the end of 1942 he again went to stay at Allen Tate's, though not this time on the lawn, and bringing with him his writer wife. The Tates and the Lowells were all engaged in literary projects. Though Lowell's was supposed to be a biography of the eighteenth-century New England minister and philosopher Jonathan Edwards, the actual result was his first book, *Land of Unlikeness*. It was set in type just before the six-month prison term he served in 1943–44, and was finally published in 1944, just after his release from the federal penitentiary. Not surprisingly, Tate wrote the introduction to the book; I shall discuss both book and introduction at a later point.

Land of Unlikeness, privately printed and given very limited distribution, received some critical attention but was essentially unnoticed. Lowell's second book, *Lord Weary's Castle*, was published in 1946 to a wave of applause; it received the Pulitzer Prize in 1947, and Lowell was well on his way to becoming both a public figure and, in more narrowly literary circles, a leader of his generation. For the last decade or so of his life, indeed, the average nonliterary bookstore in the United States reported that its shelves held only two hardcover volumes by American poets—one by Emily Dickinson, the other by Robert Lowell. He was awarded the Prize of the American Academy-National Institute of Arts and Letters in 1947; he won a Guggenheim Fellowship; he was appointed poetry consultant to the Library of Congress; and he was a member of the jury that awarded the first of the Bollingen Prizes in poetry. He was thirty years old. T. S. Eliot, William Carlos Williams, Ezra Pound, Robert Frost, and many, many others praised him in public and in private. But, as Steven Gould Axelrod nicely puts it, "Lowell's inner life was deeply troubled in the years following *Lord Weary's Castle*. . . . In the late 1940s he lost his faith, his politics, his wife, and his mind. And his poetry drifted."[1] *Life* magazine, which had joined the chorus of praise, labeled him "a shy, amiable young man" who had "reached the status of a major literary figure,"[2] but like Rod McKuen *Life* barely scratched the surface of things.

Now based in New York, and no longer quite so close to Allen Tate, Lowell found that his formalism, his conservatism, and his obsession with faintly musty rhetoric were very much out of date and out of favor. His divorce from Jean Stafford, in 1948, was distinctly bitter. When he married for the second time, in 1949, it was to Elizabeth Hardwick, not a novelist or a poet but a critic of markedly leftward beliefs (she became, much later, one of the founding pillars of the *New York Review of Books*, a secular, leftist journal). Her book, *A View of My Own*, for example, is dedicated to Philip Rahv, one of the cofounders of that once-Marxist and still radical journal, *Partisan Review*, and contains essays on the convicted murderer Caryl Chessman, who had become a rallying point for the political left, on the sociologist David Riesman, and on "The Subjection of Women." Her essay on the Catholic novelist Graham Greene speaks of the "element of snobbishness in serious Catholic writers" and asks "whether a significant picture of modern life in the last thirty years could be made from doctrinal puzzles, seminarian wit and paradox, private jokes, Roman Catholic exclusiveness."[3] The marriage lasted for roughly twenty years, was not legally dissolved until the early 1970s, and, as I have said, at his death Lowell had returned both to America and to Elizabeth Hardwick.

Lowell's mental instability, which by the early 1950s was both intense and distinctly periodic, resulted in numerous confinements in mental institutions. It is clearly important, personally and poetically, and must be clearly stated. I do not think, however, that much is to be gained from discussion of what is, in the end, no more amenable to analysis, and especially literary analysis, than any other human irrationality. Lowell was often depressed, often eccentric; his life was made difficult, and his wife and children and friends surely suffered along with him. We are his readers, not his family, and it is his poems and plays and translations with which we live—and they are *not* mad, and no more depressed than a great deal of twentieth-century art in all forms.

Lowell's third book, *The Mills of the Kavanaughs*, appeared in 1951, and was generally recognized for what it is, a confused, even a desperate attempt to move into new areas and to employ new techniques. The drifting was plainly acute in almost all aspects of Lowell's life and career. He needed to reformulate his esthetic approaches and his social viewpoints; emotionally, he had to deal with the deaths of his father, in 1951, and his mother, in 1954. He made a visit to Europe, in 1952–53; he made many visits to the firmly untraditional pöet, William Carlos Williams; he taught at the University of Iowa, the University of Cincinnati, and then for most of the 1960s at Boston University. By 1957 he was starting to write the poems that became, in 1959, the National Book Award winner—and probably his best book—*Life Studies.*These were no longer rhetorical, formal, metrical poems; it had taken Lowell, as he himself admitted, until age forty to begin to write the truly personal, deeply free poetry of his finest period. Allen Tate, interestingly, "was horrified by the manuscript of *Life Studies* and insisted that it not be published."[4]

But though temporarily free of the demons and internal divisions that had spoiled much of his early poetry and even paralyzed him as a writer for much of the 1950s, Lowell could not—as I shall explain in due course—maintain so high a level. But his career was now assured, even though at age thirty-nine, just before Lowell started the *Life Studies* poems, a cousin had informed him that he was written out and done for. In 1960 the Ford Foundation gave him a grant, trying to interest him in the creation of an opera libretto. He did not write an opera, but he did write three short plays, and he won an Obie award (for the best off-Broadway play) for one of them in 1964. He also translated Greek plays and produced a volume of "imitations"—neither translations nor original poems, but poems derived from, based on, but often sharply diverging from, their originals in other languages. By 1965, he was deeply involved in the anti-Viet Nam War movement. "I have never gotten over the horrors of American bombing," he said at the time. "For me anti-Stalinism led logically—oh, perhaps not so logically —to my being against our suppression of the Vietnamese." Invited to the White House to read his poems at a Festival of the Arts, Lowell at first accepted and then, reconsidering, refused the invitation. His long telegram to President Lyndon Johnson appeared on the front page of *The New York Times* on June 3, 1965. "I am conscience-bound to refuse your courteous invitation," he told the president. "We are in danger of imperceptibly becoming an explosive and suddenly chauvinistic nation, and may even be drifting on our way to the last nuclear ruin."

The poetry of *For the Union Dead*, which appeared in 1964, reflects this movement from the private to the public poet. There is as yet no uniformity in critical judgment of this transitional book. Some critics applaud the "density", of the volume; others, like myself, find this density overly literary and insufficiently real. (My personal copy bears the signs of extremely close, eager reading, and the final judgment, regretful but firm: "Not a really fine poem in the book.") *Near the Ocean*, which appeared in 1967, is in truth scarcely a volume of original poetry, since most of its bulk consists of imitations from Horace, Juvenal, and Dante, and the book is padded out both by drawings and by a great deal of bare white space on the pages. The original poetry too is frequently padded, but it is important to note at once that the public Lowell is not the great Lowell. There are fine passages in both these volumes, as to be sure there are fine passages in everything Lowell published—his poetic voice was as impressive as that of any poet in this century—but there is fairly general critical agreement about this book. As Richard Howard said at the time, in *Poetry* magazine, there is no question that it is "far from worthless," but also no question that it is an "odd new clutch of texts."[5] Or as R. K. Meiners nicely says, "the strain is beginning to tell."[6]

Indeed, though Lowell continued his public involvements—marching on the Pentagon in March 1967, in company with Norman Mailer, Allen Ginsberg, and many, many others, and, in 1968, both endorsing and actively working for the presidential campaign of former Senator Eugene McCarthy—four of the five volumes of poetry he published after *Near the Ocean* represent, at best, a kind of consolidation of failure. The fifth and last of the late volumes, *Day by Day*, is however in no sense a failure and may have indicated a new turning, a new and perhaps, this time, a lasting greatness But Lowell died days after its publication, and the new road was never fully traveled. The first four of these late books, which I shall refer to collectively as the *Notebook*-style poems, are in sheer bulk larger than everything Lowell put into print from 1944 to 1967, but the earlier intensity—flawed, often grotesque, and yet commanding—has been dampened, muted to a stable but monotonous skimming-off of experience, far more reportorial than deeply poetic.

And even what had seemed, for a time, to be a deep and possibly a lasting involvement in American politics culminated, in a sense, in yet another consolidation of failure: Lowell went into voluntary exile in 1970 and did not return to reside in the United States for six years. His marriage to Elizabeth Hardwick was formally ended in 1972, but he had been living with Caroline Blackwood, to whom he was married in 1972, for some while and had had a son by her in 1971. This third marriage also had wound down by early 1977. Lowell planned to teach at Harvard in the fall of that year. He made a Russian tour under the auspices of the U.S. Department of State in June of 1977, then returned to his second wife. On September 12, 1977, after a brief visit to Caroline and their child, he had a heart attack in the taxi that was taking him from Kennedy Airport, and was dead before the taxi driver knew it.

Lowell's life, intensely dramatic in an inner sense, was plainly undramatic in the usual meaning of the term. Fiercely honest, deeply intellectual, he lived in the world without being entirely of the world. His talents, in any objective overview, were as ample and compelling as those of any poet of our time, but his achievement did not measure up to his capabilities. But that is to denigrate his achievement only in some ultimate, absolute sense, for Robert Lowell—flawed, incomplete, tormented and sometimes tormenting—has left us a body of work that we who are his contemporaries have not been able to ignore, nor will it be ignorable by those who come after. There is, to use a frequently abused word, a special magic in Lowell's poetry, and in his plays, and in his translations and imitations, that forces us into attention, if not always into admiration or agreement. It is the purpose of this book to try to outline and to some extent document that magic—which, in my judgment, is itself an achievement of an imperishable sort. I will frequently be critical of Lowell; I will perhaps sound at times dismissive of this or that poem, this or that book. But I should like it to be clear from the start that Lowell is not a writer who can be condescended to or dismissed, and that it is not my intention to attempt anything thus foolishly disrespectful. My respect for Robert Lowell is absolute—but honor does not require adulation.

2

A Strained Start, a Pulitzer Prize, and a Confused Continuation: The First Three Books

Had *Land of Unlikeness*, published in 1944 when Lowell was twenty-seven, been his only volume of poetry, it would deserve (and would receive) very little attention. Indeed, like many small editions put out by small presses, *Land of Unlikeness*'s 250 copies were as much a statement of intent as an accomplishment worth notice on its own terms. Roughly half the poems were reprinted, for the most part heavily rewritten (and improved), in Lowell's second and infinitely better book, *Lord Weary's Castle*.

But of course Lowell did not stop with this probably premature first book, and it is worth examining both because its very immaturity makes extremely plain what sort of context Lowell emerged from and also because of its clues for the future. The title comes from Saint Bernard, who is quoted (but not translated from the Latin) on the title page: *"Inde anima dissimilis deo inde dissimilis est et sibi,"* or "A likeness which is no longer like its original is no longer like itself." The thrust is political: it is the United States, in its original and in its now sadly debased contemporary state, with which Lowell is concerned. That contrast, and the world war in which the country was then engaged (wrongly, to Lowell's mind), and the further contrast between "true" Christianity, which of course then meant Catholicism to Lowell, and "debased" Christianity, which meant the

Protestantism of his Puritan ancestors—these are the book's subjects. To some considerable extent, they are also the themes of much of his later work in all forms.

It needs to be very firmly kept in mind that, in 1944, poetry in English was and for some years had been dominated by the work, the ideas, and even the attitudes of T. S. Eliot, then but fifty-six years old. There were contradictory stirrings and there were literary rebels, but for most of Lowell's generation—as for the generation of Allen Tate, Lowell's early mentor—Eliot was model and inevitable starting-ground. In introducing *Land of Unlikeness*, Tate invoked Eliot almost as poets once invoked the sacred Muses: "There is no other poetry today quite like this. T. S. Eliot's recent prediction that we should soon see a return to formal and even intricate metres and stanzas was coming true, before he made it, in the verse of Robert Lowell."[1] It was Eliot's poetry that usually had the deepest and the most lasting impact. But his ringing prose formulations sometimes had as much or even more effect. In 1928 Eliot had proclaimed his "general point of view" to be "classicist in literature, royalist in politics, and anglo-catholic in religion."[2] Eliot's "classicism" extended to Dante and most signally to the then still-neglected Metaphysical poets, John Donne above all others. So pervasive was the impact of Eliot's stance that, at Lowell's death in 1977, he was working on a long essay on Dante. But the impact went still deeper. Eliot's 1921 essay on the Metaphysical poets contained the following brilliantly phrased and yet, for a young poet a quarter of a century later, extremely dangerous formulation:

. . . Something had happened to the mind of England between the time of Donne or Lord Herbert of Cherbury and the time of Tennyson and Browning. . . . Tennyson and Browning are poets, and they think; but they do not feel their thought as immediately as the odour of a rose. A thought to Donne was an experience; it modified his sensibility. *When a poet's mind is perfectly equipped for its work, it is constantly amalgamating disparate experience;* the ordinary man's experience is chaotic, irregular, fragmentary . . . ; in the mind of the poet these experiences are always forming new wholes.[3] [italics mine]

Lowell tried to be the poet T. S. Eliot had described— and "chaotic" and "fragmentary" are two apt words for the poetry that resulted. His impressionability was close to disastrous. "When I was twenty and learning to write," Lowell later explained, "Allen Tate, Eliot, [R.P.] Blackmur, and [Yvor] Winters, and all those people were very much news. You waited for their essays, and when a good critical essay came out it had the excitement of a new imaginative work."

There were reasons, and some of them good reasons, for Lowell's fascination with "amalgamating disparate experience." He was himself such an amalgam, a native American grossly dissatisfied with contemporary America, a Protestant turned against the religion of his ancestors, a son who in good measure loathed his parents. One of the reviewers of this first book commented, accurately, that "In Lowell's *Land of Unlikeness* there is nothing loved unless it be its repellence . . . and the fight produces not a tension but a gritting."[4] Lowell was also decidedly an intellectual, a person who apprehended reality as much in books and magazines as in the flesh. It is hardly accidental that his career was to some extent a veering from one literary influence, one mentor, to another, or that *Life Studies*, probably his best book, is not only the simplest but, along with *Day by Day*, the most intensely personal he ever produced. Hayden Carruth, himself a very fine poet, says in a long review of Lowell's *Near the Ocean* that "the primal creative act . . . is something prior to poetry. Before a man can create a poem he must create a poet."[5]

> Christ's bread and beauty came by you,
> Celestial Hoyden, when our Lord
> Gave up the weary Ghost and died,

> You shook a sword
> From his torn side.

These lines, from a poem entitled "On the Eve of the Feast of the Immaculate Conception, 1942," are typical of the dangers involved in creating a poet, and simultaneously his poetry, out of an amalgamation of disparate experience. "Celestial Hoyden," as a way of self-consciously overintellectualizing the Virgin Mary, turning what is theologically real into something poetically false and strained, is clearly a product of the mind and not of the man. The pun on "Ghost" is rather drearily an echo of John Donne; the strictly literary violence of "shook" in the last of these quoted lines is clearly derivative of the stale, forced lines of Allen Tate's poetry.[6] The lack of any human center makes for a striking lack of literary balance. Even Lowell's good friend Randall Jarrell said of poems like this that they were "[Lowell's] variant of Tolstoy's motto, 'Make it strange,' . . . 'Make it grotesque.' "[7]

> The maimed man stopped and slung me on his back:
> My borrowed car flopped quacking in the flood,
> It foundered in the lowest bog.
> Man, why was it your rotten fabric broke?
> "Brother, I fattened a caged beast on blood
> And knowledge had let the cat out of the bag."

This is the final stanza of "A Suicidal Nightmare," one of the poems not perpetuated in *Lord Weary's Castle*. It is not hard to see why, for though there is genuine power in such lines, though there is authentic feeling and thought, there is also no personal voice, no sense that the particular poet is here totally in command of the particular images and statements of this particular poem. On the one hand, it does not matter that we are not told who "the maimed man" is, or why the car is "borrowed." The lines are vivid, and vividness excuses many sins. But when that borrowed car "flops," and then "quacks," the disparate experiences T. S. Eliot wrote of do not come together into what he called "new wholes." They break apart, instead, into merely willed "wholes" that are, alas, no better than the "ordinary man's experience" of which Eliot also wrote. Cars do not turn into ducks because a would-be poet says they do: there is much much more to the writing of poetry than that.

Nor does insistence help. Consider the following passages, one from the sonnet entitled "Salem" (a poem reproduced unchanged in *Lord Weary's Castle*), one from the sonnet entitled "Concord" (reproduced but substantially changed), which follows immediately afterward in both books:

> In Salem seasick spindrift drifts or skips
> To the canvas flapping on the seaward panes
> Until the knitting seaman stabs at ships
> Nosing like sheep of Morpheus through his brain's
> Asylum.

>   Crucifix,
> How can your whited spindling arms transfix
> Mammon's unbridled industry, the lurch
> For forms to harness Heraclitus' stream!

Virtually everything is excessive, and therefore ineffective, in these lines. The very sounds are excessive: the *s* alliteration in "Salem" is so heavy that it seems parodistic. The syntax grows so clotted that it stretches out and virtually snaps: by the time we reach "Nosing like sheep of Morpheus through his brain's/ Asylum," we are not struggling with the poetry but with the rather more basic problem of pronoun reference. It is probably the sailor's brain—but might it be Morpheus's? And at that point poetry ceases to be possible.

And both these passages, the second especially, highlight yet another obstacle to the kind of heaped-up, jungle-dense poetry that Lowell would like to think he is writing, namely the over-use—and the over-facile use—of symbolic allusions. As the distinguished classicist William Arrowsmith wrote in reviewing Lowell's third book, "Persephone and Hades [but read also, Morpheus, Mammon, or Heraclitus] are rich enough symbols in themselves that they must be carefully controlled if they are not to become obscure. . . . [Lowell] proceeds, characteristically, to pack his symbols so that his sim- plicities assume a complexity which wrecks them."[8] Again, Lowell's excesses are not simply out of control, not simply young and overenthusiastic, but are in my judgment part of an overall and lifelong difficulty. The very intensity of his drive away from simplicity, indeed, his apparent need to escape into complexity, to hide in complexity, seems to me to indicate that his excessiveness is the farthest thing from accidental. No smoke screen of erudite allusions will in fact work, any more than a bristling hedge of violent verbs will work, or a torrent of alliteration. "Before a man can create a poem he must create a poet"—and he can create a poet only out of himself, out of his own materials. It cannot be done with borrowed tools, borrowed symbols, or borrowed any- thing else.

And, in this first book, Catholicism seems to me precisely a borrowed symbol. Lowell is so insistent, so nearly hysterical, in his attacks on Puritan Protestantism and in his loud advocacy of anything and everything Catholic, that he utterly fails to persuade—or even to interest—the reader. He sings to the Christ child of a new baby, dead, and then says to that dead baby, "Child, the Mayflower rots/ In your poor bred-out stock." Entitled "The Boston Nativity" (and not reprinted in *Lord Weary's Castle*), the poem is almost embarrassing, so fierce and two-dimensional are its attacks and its celebrations alike. "So, child, unclasp your fists," he commands the dead baby, "And clap for Freedom and Democracy;/ No matter, child, if the Ark Royal lists/

Into the sea;/ Soon the Leviathan/ Will sprout American."
Again, casual allusion to a sunken British naval vessel,
the Ark Royal, cannot support a symbolic allusion so
massive as Leviathan. And, in truth, there is no more
reason to believe his extravagant assertion that whales
will be domesticated to the American flag—that is, we
do not believe it even enough for purposes of ironic
disbelief—than there is to credit the claim, earlier in
the poem, that "If Baby asks for gifts at birth,/ Santa will
hang/ Bones of democracy/ Upon the Christmas Tree."
For a supposedly religious poem, "The Boston Nativity"
rants and raves distinctly too much and displays overall
far more negativism than it does belief. From the
"unchristian carollings" of line 2 to "the benighted
Magian," namely Santa Claus, of line 33, the poem is a
continual attack. And the belief that finally arrives, in
the final couplet (lines 35–36), is both too little and much
too late: "Jesus, the Maker of this holiday,/ Ungirds his
loins' eternal clay." R. P. Blackmur, a critic friendly to
Lowell, once said with great charity that "Lowell is
distraught about religion."[9] I think it would be more
accurate to say that Lowell desperately wanted to be
both religious and a religious poet, but lacked true
vocation as evidently as he lacked deep belief. "It
frequently happens that when Mr. Lowell is dealing
with a religious subject something seems to go wrong
with his verse" wrote Marius Bewley. "A religious theme
is usually a signal for intolerable strain."[10] Bewley is not
a critic friendly to Lowell, but here he is inescapably
right.

    Before we leave *Land of Unlikeness*, let me em-
phasize that there are good lines and a few good poems
in the book. The good lines, however, seem to flash out
at the reader from wallowing immaturities and do not
last long enough to raise whole poems to their singular
level. For example, "Christmas Eve in the Time of
War," subtitled "A Capitalist Meditates by a Civil War

Monument" (heavily revised and sharply cut, as well as
retitled in *Lord Weary's Castle*, where it appears as
"Christmas Eve Under Hooker's Statue"), begins with
two terse, effective lines: "Tonight a blackout. Twenty
years ago/ I strung my stocking on the tree . . ." But the
clotted, stale, bombastic rhetoric immediately takes over:
". . .—if Hell's/ Inactive sting stuck in the stocking's
toe,/ Money would draw it out. Stone generals . . .
[etc.]" Similarly, the first poem in the book, "The Park
Street Cemetery" (not reprinted in *Lord Weary's Castle*),
begins crisply, then decays with great rapidity: "In back
of the Athenaeum, only/ The dead are poorer. Here
frayed/ Cables wreathe the spreading obelisk . . . " And
the few good poems, finally, are not in Lowell's own
voice; they are, rather, fine student work, aping an
assortment of earlier writers. "Satan's Confession" begins
quite beautifully:

> The laurels are cut down,
> The Son of Darkness mourns;
> > Old Adam's funeral wreath,
> > Once crossed with death,
> Is Jesus' crown,
> King Jesus' Crown of thorns.

Again, this is lovely—but it is not really Lowell, or
indeed any twentieth-century poet, but an extremely
clever pastiche of Lowell's elders and betters. Not
susprisingly, the poem is not reprinted in his second
book. Or take the third stanza of "The Drunken Fish-
erman" (reprinted almost unchanged in *Lord Weary's
Castle*), which has a delicacy and a restraint rare in this
poet—so rare, indeed, that the lines simply are not
Lowell's own, but are borrowed attributes:

> Once fishing was a rabbit's foot:
> O wind blow cold, O wind blow hot,
> Let suns stay in or suns step out:
> Life danced a jig on the sperm-whale's spout:

> The fisher's fluent and obscene
> Catches kept his conscience clean.
> Children, the raging memory drools
> Over the glory of past pools.

I cannot blame Lowell for reprinting, nor for not revising, so pleasant a poem. But this sort of elegance was neither properly his, nor was it a possible pathway to open out new territories, new approaches. For all its delightfulness, it is a dead end, and Lowell knew it. The poem was reprinted almost unchanged, but its style and its tone were not used again.

Lord Weary's Castle seems an almost impossible leap forward for a poet as immature and strained, as clotted and precious and uncontrolled, as Lowell had been only two years earlier. It makes sense to find that Lowell had a good deal of help. His friend Randall Jarrell "carefully went over the manuscript of *Lord Weary's Castle*, providing Lowell with a heavy marginal annotation which explained and evaluated individual poems, lines, and words with marvelous subtlety and rightness. Although Jarrell never suggested particular changes (except occasionally in the matter of punctuation), Lowell systematically altered lines and words disapproved by his friend . . . "[11] All the same, the poems and the achievement are Lowell's and no one else's—and *Lord Weary's Castle* was and is so very fine a book that it "established him with one shot as a leader of his generation."[12] Many critics went even farther, seeing Lowell as "the present best hope of American poetry."[13]

The first lines of the first poem in the book show how much has been gained:

> There mounts in squalls a sort of rusty mire,
> Not ice, not snow, to leaguer the Hôtel
> De Ville, where braced pig-iron dragons grip
> The blizzard to their rigor mortis.

This is not easy poetry, but it is vastly more open, and very much easier. Image material is now subordinated to theme; it no longer runs wild, and the poem no longer runs to excess. The breath line has become shorter, too, which is yet another important step toward a more open, a more natural poetic. The movement within these shorter-breathed lines, too, is distinctly more relaxed, at times even gracious. And formally, as well, these lines and the poems that follow show an easing of tradition's iron grip. Virtually all the poems in *Land of Unlikeness* are stanzaic in form, or are sonnets, but this first poem and a good many of the poems in *Lord Weary's Castle* are what musicians call "through composed." That is, instead of using structural devices of a repeating nature, like the stanza, the poet allows the structure of the poem to evolve organically, as it were, out of the poem's own imperatives. It is a freer principle; it is also a harder process to control and requires much more daring, as well as much more skill. Finally, though I do not want to discuss metrics until we reach *Life Studies*, where it seems to me of crucial importance, Lowell's metrics too show signs of easing in *Lord Weary's Castle*. He is, in short, not only a much better poet here, he is also a much looser and freer-moving poet.

There are some extraordinary successes. Randall Jarrell's judgment seems to me accurate: "One or two of these poems, I think, will be read as long as men remember English."[14] There will be time enough to consider some of the continuing problems after we look, in some detail, at one of the longest but not one of the best-known poems in the book, the four-part, five-page "Between the Porch and the Altar." It strikes me as exemplary of his newfound powers; detailed discussion of this ambitious poem should help stake out the boundaries of his new success.

The poem's title seems to be a conscious echoing of the two divisions, "The Church-Porch" and "The

Church," of George Herbert's *The Temple*, one of the classics of seventeenth-century Metaphysical poetry. (Lord Herbert of Cherbury, mentioned by T.S. Eliot in a passage cited earlier, is George Herbert's older brother; the younger man, and better poet, was a clergyman and something of a recluse.) The four sections are entitled "Mother and Son," "Adam and Eve," "Katherine's Dream," and finally "At the Altar." Here is the opening portion of the first section, "Mother and Son":

> Meeting his mother makes him lose ten years,
> Or is it twenty? Time, no doubt, has ears
> That listen to the swallowed serpent, wound
> Into its bowels, but he thinks no sound
> Is possible before her, he thinks the past
> Is settled. It is honest to hold fast
> Merely to what one sees with one's own eyes
> When the red velvet curves and haunches rise
> To blot him from the pretty driftwood fire's
> Façade of welcome.

The first thing to note, I think, is the extraordinary economy of these lines, which move tautly, firmly toward an organized presentation, a controlled presentation. There is none of the earlier straining after isolated effects, the rather desperate reaching for some uniquely startling image (or images) in each and every line. The form is the iambic pentameter couplet, and it is as required closely rhymed, but it is not the end-stopped form of the couplet used in the eighteenth century (most notably by Alexander Pope). Not only are the couplets enjambed (that is, run-on rather than end-stopped), which deemphasizes the regular rhyming, there is also cross (or slant) rhyme within the couplet. That is, "wound/ Into its bowels" uses the rhyme-word "wound" to rhyme both with "sound," at the end of the following line, and (partially) with "bowels," in the middle of the line. And rhyme thus becomes a technique of heightened complexity and interest. So too, only a few lines further on, with "the past/Is settled." Nor is the lurching half-pause at the end of the first line, "ten years,/ Or is it twenty?", used mechanically, as it was apt to be in the first book. Lowell here gives himself the time, and the amplitude, to characterize the people in the poem; earlier, he kept rushing from one wild generalization to another. The mother, a ripely middle-aged matron, is presented to us dramatically, as "red velvet curves and haunches." We see how carefully she has staged this meeting—"the pretty driftwood fire"—and yet we are also informed of the staginess, by the neatly compressed phrase, "Façade of welcome." Not true welcome, but only a façade. And, further, we are shown the effect of all this charade on the son: as his mother rises to greet him, even the façade of welcome is blotted out by her insistent presence.

Let me step back from "Between the Porch and the Altar" for just a moment, in order to emphasize by comparison both how difficult such poetry is to write and how necessary some such approach was for poets of Lowell's generation. The major problem, once again, was how to escape from, how to move forward and past, the poetry of T. S. Eliot. Weldon Kees (1914–1955), three years Lowell's senior, never quite managed it. He was caught in Eliot's orbit and essentially stayed there, trapped. The closest he came to breaking away, however, was in passages like the following, from his late poem, "Saratoga Ending," roughly contemporaneous with the poems of *Lord Weary's Castle*:

> I lie here in the dark, trying to remember
> What my life has taught me. The driveway lights blur
> In the rain. A rubber-tired metal cart goes by,
> Followed by a nurse; and something rattles
> Like glasses being removed after
> A party is over and the guests have gone.

> Test tubes, beakers, graduates, thermometers—
> Companions of these years that I no longer count.[15]

Less formal than Lowell, Kees is nevertheless using a very similar approach, attempting to take the intense, compressed urbanity of Eliot beyond what Eliot did with it. Just as in the passage from "Between the Porch and the Altar," we see "disparate experience" linked in a pattern both more common and ordinary and also less portentous than in Eliot's poetry. And yet, though Kees was able to move even this far from Eliot only in a very few poems, and usually only in portions of those poems, he has not moved quite so far as has Lowell. The overgeneralized portentousness of "What my life has taught me," the overinsistent ordinariness of the list of objects—"Test tubes, beakers, graduates, thermometers"—and the merely flat descriptiveness of "a rubber-tired metal cart," all suggest the stifling power of Eliot's example. Kees lacked Lowell's strength, and in part knowing that he lacked it, and therefore could never resolve his poetic inadequacies, he committed suicide. Again, it is the farthest thing from easy to escape the towering presence of a predecessor—in any art. How many musicians did Beethoven swallow? How many painters are struggling, still, to escape from Picasso? Lowell's achievement, in short, was a remarkable one.

To return to "Between the Porch and the Altar": we see the son cringing, confronted with his powerful mother, and at the same time cringing at himself for cringing. And we are also presented with an important further stage in the characterization of the mother, given to us in strictly image-form:

> Nothing shames
> Him more than this uncoiling, counterfeit
> Body presented as an idol. It
> Is something in a circus, big as life,
> The painted dragon, a mother and a wife
> With flat glass eyes pushed at him on a stick . . .

The sequence of images is beautifully controlled. There is, first, the adjective "uncoiling," obviously snakelike and yet immediately both retreated from and changed by "counterfeit," at the same time suggesting some of the fiscal links between mother and son and building on the snake image with an oblique reference to the primordial snake, Satan himself, the very model of a "counterfeit body." Lowell immediately narrows this latter reference by "idol," which limits us to a pagan context in which Satan has no place. He reinforces this new image with the circus reference, which still further mocks the mother—an "idol" is, in this Christian poem, something very much less worthy than even a Satanic reference, but a "circus" is distinctly lower still on the moral scale—and then completes the entire sequence by combining both pagan and circus references with the snake image he began with. The mother thus becomes a "painted dragon . . . with flat glass eyes"—and how delicately he has managed the whole thing! Further, "painted" conveys something basic about the woman, as well as helping us to visualize the fake dragon she truly is, just as the "glass eyes" tell us something, too, about her human as well as about her snake-and-dragon nature. Note too how quietly "big as life" does its work of characterization, since "big as life" is all the mother in fact needs to be, once the son, though ostensibly mature, has been shrunk back to childhood size (in lines I have not here quoted). And then the final couplet—here very firmly end-stopped, for emphasis—transforms the son too into a kind of snake figure. After "With flat glass eyes pushed at him on a stick," Lowell continues, "The human mover crawls to make them click." It is the son's crawling, if I read this passage correctly, which produces that "click" in the snake-mother's eyes, which triggers the rapacious and plainly inhuman (or, more accurately, nonhuman) reaction.

Lowell then ties up these savage characterizations,

and this first section of the poem, with the same deft
precision and newfound ease:

> . . . the schoolboy kneels
> To ask the benediction of the hand,
> Lifted as though to motion him to stand,
> Dangling its watch-chain on the Holy Book—
> A little golden snake that mouths a hook.

That watch-chain snake of gold is, of course, literally the
mother's jewelry. But after the long development of the
mother-as-reptile image, it is I think impossible to feel
that the "hook" with which the section ends is merely
a thing of decorative import.

Section two, "Adam and Eve," opens with the
following brilliant passage:

> The farmer sizzles on his shaft all day.
> He is content and centuries away
> From white-hot Concord, and he stands on guard.
> Or is he melting down like sculptured lard?

The poem is opened out, here, with singular mastery.
The "farmer" of the first line, which line is made self-
contained by the period that ends it and thus seals it up
for the moment, can perhaps be a real farmer as he
"sizzles," though even that is doubtful. But once we
know that he is on a "shaft," and even more as we learn
that he "sizzles . . . all day," he is subtly transformed
into what he in fact is, namely a statue of a farmer. What
sort of farmer? Line two tells us that he is "centuries
away"; line three tells us that he is a Concord farmer
and "stands on guard." The reference to the Revolutionary farmers of Concord is obvious. We can then
appreciate the delicate power with which Lowell has
fused weather heat ("sizzles") with battle heat ("white-
hot Concord"), as also the neat ironical undercutting of
"stands on guard" by the following "melting down like
sculptured lard." The reader cannot help but trust the
poet, in the face of such tightly controlled writing;

indeed, he finds himself obliged to relish the poet's work
when the irony is so deliciously driven home.

Section two continues:

> His hand is crisp and steady on the plough.
> I quarreled with you, but am happy now
> To while [wile?] away my life for your unrest
> Of terror. Never to have lived is best;
> Man tasted Eve with death. I taste my wife
> And children while I hold your hands. I knife
> Their names into this elm. What is exempt?

The Revolutionary War statue, erected after all in
celebration of heroes who were truly heroic and truly
deserving of celebration, is now given to us without
irony, "crisp and steady on the plough." But the irony
returns at once, this time directed at the "son" of the
first part, who is now exposed to us in his version of the
ancient game of "Adam and Eve." He is with a woman
clearly not his wife (though I must admit I have never
been able to understand "your unrest of terror"; whether
Lowell or I am at fault I cannot say), and just as clearly
not his mother. But much the same fear of and hostility
to women that we saw in the first section is vividly
present here, in an erotic rather than a maternal relationship. Nor, equally plainly, is that juxtaposition of
sexual woman and mother woman an accidental matter.
Fear and hostility are the hallmarks of all male-female
relationships, Lowell insists: "Man tasted Eve with
death." Again, furthermore, the man is part boy, cutting
names into a tree with a knife. And the boy-man who
says, with rather contemptible self-pity, "Never to have
lived is best," is implicitly contrasted with "crisp and
steady" man who once inhabited Concord. And

> . . . They lied,
> My cold-eyed seedy fathers when they died,
> Or rather threw their lives away, to fix
> Sterile, forbidding nameplates on the bricks
> Above a kettle. Jesus rest their souls!

It has been said that, could Martin Luther, the founder
of Protestantism, have foreseen the "pale negations" of
Boston Unitarianism, he would have been more likely
to cut off his right hand than to allow it to nail his anti-
Papal theses to the door of that famous church in
Wittenberg. Lowell insists, here, that after those "crisp
and steady" farmers came a stream of pompous, sterile,
material-oriented men. The heroes of Concord threw
their lives into the balance, to achieve freedom and
independence, but these men "threw their lives away"
and for nothing more elevated than "forbidding name-
plates on the bricks/Above a kettle." And after this
invocation of whatever spiritual solace may be available,
for such unspiritual beings (I am inclined to take this
invocation seriously, as I cannot take seriously somewhat
similar phrases in *Land of Unlikeness*), this deeply
unerotic second part ends, returning to "Adam and Eve":

> You cry for help. Your market-basket rolls
> With all its baking apples in the lake.
> You watch the whorish slither of a snake
> That chokes a duckling. When we try to kiss,
> Our eyes are slits and cringing, and we hiss;
> Scales glitter on our bodies as we fall.
> The Farmer melts upon his pedestal.

Just as there is no real help for the "cold-eyed seedy
fathers," so too is there none for this as yet unnamed
woman, involved with a man of this sort. She feels the
quasidemonic snake, choking a duckling, to be "whor-
ish," as of course she also feels herself to be. Both their
snakelike, Satan-affected natures emerge as they "hiss,"
and we are told that, as they tumble into the bushes
(and also into the theological "fall"), there are "scales
[that] glitter on our bodies." And, at this unenlightening
spectacle, "The Farmer melts" in sorrow and misery,
forced to watch what his descendants have sunk (or
fallen) to.

The third part of the poem, "Katherine's Dream,"
is I think the most powerful of all the four sections.
Katherine is the "other woman," the miserable mistress,
and the poetic fabric is so tightly woven, here, that it is
difficult to deal with it in smaller segments. This section
begins with lines that in a sense echo T. S. Eliot's
portrait of adulterous love in *The Waste Land*, but also
transform that famous portrait of contemporary deca-
dence into something very much more commonplace:

> It must have been a Friday. I could hear
> The top-floor typist's thunder and the beer
> That you brought in cases hurt my head;
> I'd sent the pillows flying from my bed,
> I hugged my knees together and I gasped.
> The dangling telephone receiver rasped
> Like someone in a dream who cannot stop
> For breath or logic till his victim drop
> To darkness and the sheets.

She lives in rented, distinctly unpalatial quarters, a
relative poverty neatly juxtaposed against his traditional
(that is, unearned and more than likely undeserved)
affluence, which is exhibited and faintly mocked by the
disclosure that he brings "beer . . . in cases." They drink
too much, which is dreamlike, or perhaps nightmarelike,
but is also reality—as is the abandoned, "dangling
telephone receiver." The voice on the other end of the
line, it is indicated a bit further along, is that of her
father, "who had kept/ Your guilty presents but cut off
my hair." The double entendre of "drop/ To darkness
and the sheets," which blends death and sex without
any distinction being made between them, fits perfectly
with the view of male-female relationships that has come
before. Indeed, the dropped "victim" of one "who cannot
stop" underlines this identification of murder and the
act of love.

After we hear more of her hypocritical father, who
"really doesn't care" but is—he says, obviously lying—

driven to drink by "my dishonor," she walks "through snow into St. Patrick's yard." And there, though "none/ Is friendless in this crowd,"

> I stand aside and marvel; for a while
> The winter sun is pleasant and it warms
> My heart with love for others, but the swarms
> Of penitents have dwindled. I begin
> To cry and ask God's pardon for our sin.

Neither nature nor church can help her: it would be hard to feel more alone, and lonelier:

> Where are you? You were with me and are gone.
> All the forgiven couples hurry on
> To dinner and their nights, and none will stop.
> I run about in circles till I drop
> Against a padlocked bulkhead in a yard
> Where faces redden and the snow is hard.

Others couple, hurrying off from church, back to their dinners and then to "their nights," and are eternally secure, "forgiven." But she and he are not coupled, though they couple, and all she can do, in the dreamlike image that ends this section, is "run about in circles till I drop." Animal lust has in a sense trapped her in the snow exactly like a caged-in animal; she is "padlocked," and even the snow is unforgiving and "hard."

The fourth part, finally, entitled "At the Altar," ends with the male character at a nightclub and then at a church. "I sit at a gold table with my girl/Whose eyelids burn with brandy," it begins, then shows him thinking of himself as "a fallen Christmas tree," an image that neatly revives the boy-man theme of the earlier sections. Driving off, he whispers cravenly "in her ear,"

> You know
> I want to leave my mother and my wife,
> You wouldn't have me tied to them for life . . .

His self-exposure is vivid. He sees himself as wanting

to be "decent," and yet manages at the same time, somehow, to blame the mistress for his predicament—which predicament, we are casually informed, includes the deadly identification of "my mother and my wife," again without the slightest distinction made between them. All he can do, plainly, is whine. And then at church, where a priest is saying Mass, "the Day/ Breaks with its lightning on the man of clay,/ *Dies amara valde* [the great bitterness of the day]." Lowell swiftly and inexorably ties together all the strands of this bitter poem in a poisonously bitter, and powerfully dramatic, ending:

> Here the Lord
> Is Lucifer in harness: hand on sword,
> He watches me for Mother, and will turn
> The bier and baby-carriage where I burn.

The watchful angel, supervising as Adam and Eve leave Paradise, the Garden of Eden, here is transmuted into God as an infernal baby-sitter, employed by the mother. It is a kind of mad incarnation of what psychology tells us happens with infantile parental injunctions, transformed by time and maturity into a superego, a kind of built-in parent to walk the rest of our lives alongside us, whispering and commanding the necessary rules and regulations. The man lacks courage to *be*—and so, whether as a child in his carriage or a presumed adult on his funeral bier, he will necessarily "burn."

I have not dwelled so much on "Between the Porch and the Altar," to the necessary neglect of other fine poems, because I think it the single best poem in *Lord Weary's Castle*. It is however among the best—in 1947 Lowell informed an anthologist that he himself considered it one of the five best poems in the book, and as late as 1976 he still ranked it very high[16]—and its length permits a display of Lowell's structural skills, as well as his other new poetic strengths. The most famous and most frequently discussed poem in the book is probably

"Mr. Edwards and the Spider," and despite some lumbering and stiffness in the middle sections, it is a magisterial performance, glowing with power and controlled passion. "I saw the spiders marching through the air," it begins, "Swimming from tree to tree that mildewed day/ In latter August when the hay/ Came creaking to the barn." That opening could not be bettered, to my mind; there is very little poetry that soars to such levels of realized drama, both emotional and intellectual. Lowell's obsession with Jonathan Edwards, one of the great divines and great natural and moral philosophers of early New England, creates magnificent poetry, as it also does in the oddly oriental poem that is also about Edwards, "After the Surprising Conversions." (The latter title is drawn from Edwards's own account of the same name, which details with great passion what today strikes us as revolting religious excess—tiny children locking themselves in closets and screaming for hours on end about their great sins, and so on.)

Lowell's failures in this second book do not need to detain us very long. They are not very different from the failures of his first book. Indeed, it would be nothing short of miraculous if they were very different, with only two years between the two books. "At the Indian Killer's Grave," for example, which toward its close has eleven lines in his best new manner (beginning "Here/ A clutter of Bible and weeping willows guards/ The stern Colonial magistrates . . ."), opens with the overwrought hysteria of *Land of Unlikeness*:

> Behind King's Chapel what the earth has kept
> Whole from the jerking noose of time extends
> Its dark enigma to Jehosaphat;
> Or will King Philip plait
> The just man's scalp in the wailing valley!

Similarly, "The Holy Innocents" offers us "King Herod

shrieking vengeance at the curled/ Up knees of Jesus
choking in the air," and "Colloquy in Black Rock" opens
with all the stops open and the poetic instrument blaring:

> Here the jack-hammer jabs into the ocean;
> My heart, you race and stagger and demand
> More blood-gangs for your nigger-brass percussions,
> Till I, the stunned machine of your devotion,
> Clanging upon this cymbal of a hand,
> Am rattled screw and footloose.

Credulity is not simply strained here, but overthrown.
As he did so often in his first book, Lowell jumps on his
poetic horse and rides off in all directions at the same
time. The immensely literary, immensely praised, and
almost as frequently damned "The Quaker Graveyard in
Nantucket"[17] once again contains some magnificent lines,
and one line in particular, "The stream flows down under
the druid tree," has a strange and haunting lyricism.
But it also, and mostly, hammers and smashes in Lowell's
worst early manner: "Who will dance/ The mast-lashed
master of Leviathans/ Up from this field of Quakers in
their unstoned graves?" It may well be true, as Jerome
Mazzaro nicely says, that "the poem outlines man's
dominion on earth as assigned by God in Genesis."[18]
And it also may well be true that, as Steven Gould
Axelrod claims, in this poem "Lowell constructed a
verbal structure to contain the profound antinomies of
his own being."[19] But if the poetry is hollow, what does
it matter?

> Sailors, who pitch this portent at the sea
> Where dreadnaughts shall confess
> Its hell-bent deity,
> When you are powerless
> To sand-bag this Atlantic bulwark, faced
> By the earth-shaker [Poseidon, sea-god], green, un-
>   wearied, chaste
> In his steel scales: ask for no Orphean lute
> To pluck life back. The guns of the steeled fleet

Recoil and then repeat
The hoarse salute.

This is the Homerically intended close of the poem's
first part. The trouble with leaning on Homer, Poseidon,
Herman Melville, or Orpheus in this name-dropping
way, as I have said before, is that the mere mention of
an evocative name evokes only that name—nothing
more. It is very literary, but it is also largely verbal.
This is a poem written in memory of his cousin, Warren
Winslow, "dead at sea." We know that Lowell had
himself twice tried to enlist in the Navy early in World
War Two, but had twice been rejected. Ultimately, his
conscience, or perhaps more accurately the public side
of his conscience, led him to defy the Selective Service
draft and to serve six months in prison as a conscientious
objector. "The Quaker Graveyard in Nantucket" at-
tempts to work from the other side of his conscience,
the private side as it were, and to deal with Lowell's
feelings for (and perhaps also his guilt about the death
of) his cousin. But whether he was in fact close to Warren
Winslow and wrote the poem out of that intimacy, or
whether he wrote out of some combination of family
feeling and personal feeling, does not in my view matter.
Whether it is personal or familial, whether it is philosophical or historical, or any combination thereof, it
seems to me plain that the poem touches him in areas
where, at the time he wrote it, poetry itself was in good
part blocked, just as it had been largely blocked in his
first book. Accordingly, rather than being a genuinely
embodied expression of Lowell's concerns, an expression
fleshed out with life and vitality and consequently with
true meaning, poems of this sort seem to me filled only
with intention, and largely inert. There is still far too
much of this sort of thing in *Lord Weary's Castle*—but
then Lowell was only twenty-nine when he published
it, and we can be thankful that he had another three
decades still to go.

There is I think virtually total critical agreement
that Lowell's third book, *The Mills of the Kavanaughs*,
published in 1951, is with the exception of some of the
six short poems that accompany the very long title
poem—some, but not all—a total disaster. Not surprisingly, this long narrative work had its origin in a poem
called "The Kavanaughs of the Mills," written in 1937
when Lowell had camped out at Allen Tate's house. It
is on the face of it understandable that an ambitious
poet, recently the winner of a Pulitzer Prize and the
recipient of many honors, should wish to cap his achievement with a long poem that would solidify his reputation.
Unfortunately, Lowell sadly mistook his own gifts: despite a few passages worth reading, "The Mills of the
Kavanaughs" is best passed over in merciful silence. It
marks an important stage in Lowell's ultimate movement
out of Catholicism and grandiosity; since he worked it
up for publication, it probably represented something
he had to overcome before he could move on. But it is
simply not worth our time. Lowell later called it,
disparagingly, "an obscure, rather Elizabethan" poem,
but even that is too kind.

The six short poems are, as I have indicated, by no
means consistently good, though all are I think better
than the title poem. "Falling Asleep Over the Aeneid"
is a deft set-piece that has been reasonably termed "a
dazzling pastiche of Virgil"[20] and rather extravagantly
called as good "a poem about power and the self as any
I can recall."[21] Unlike Wallace Stevens's great "Sunday
Morning," the poem with which it seems to consciously
challenge comparison,[22] "Falling Asleep Over the
Aeneid" leaves no emotional residue, no leftover warmth
or passion. Stevens writes, magnificently,

> Is there no change of death in paradise?
> Does ripe fruit never fall? Or do the boughs
> Hang always heavy in that perfect sky,
> Unchanging, yet so like our perishing earth . . .

Stevens is formal, deeply ruminative; he knows how to mix, effortlessly and delightfully, simple reality and profound speculation: " . . . late/ Coffee and oranges in a sunny chair,/ And the green freedom of a cockatoo/ Upon a rug . . . " But the cool artifice—admirable, deft, but cool for all that—is obvious in Lowell's poem from even the first few lines:

> The sun is blue and scarlet on my page,
> And *yuck-a, yuck-a, yuck-a, yuck-a,* rage
> The yellowhammers mating.

Four "yuck-a's" are roughly two too many; scarlet carries a faintly precious, unreal aura; and "rage" is just a bit too much. It all gets to be much too much, barely four lines further along, when we are told that the Trojan "files/ Clank by the body of my comrade—miles/ Of filings!" As even Lowell's friend, Randall Jarrell, wrote of the long title poem we have essentially ignored, sometimes "the poem becomes so academic and clumsy that one is astonished."[23] There are to be sure many better things in this poem. But what in the end it portrays, despite its epigraph, which asserts that it is about "An old man in Concord [who] forgets to go to morning service . . . [and] falls asleep, while reading Vergil, and dreams that he is Aeneas at the funeral of Pallas, an Italian prince," is not the old man or anything he dreams, but rather Lowell's own reactions to the poet Virgil. Stevens too writes of an older person, and he too mixes allusion and reflection, description and natural movements, but his poem not only gives us the old woman's feelings, but leaves us with reflections totally appropriate to her inner state: "We live in an old chaos of the sun,/ Or old dependency of day and night,/ Or island solitude, unsponsored, free,/ Of that wide water, inescapable." Lowell gives us a bit of brilliant literary criticism:

It is I, I hold
His sword to keep from falling, for the dust
On the stuffed birds is breathless, for the bust
Of young Augustus weighs on Vergil's shelf:
It scowls into my glasses at itself.

There is the odor of library dust about these lines,
beautifully tempered but neutral. Lowell's better direction, as I shall indicate in the next chapter, is far more
inward than this polished and fundamentally unstirring
verse.

The last of the shorter poems, and the only other
one I want to briefly discuss here, is "Thanksgiving's
Over," which some critics term inert, but which Jerome
Mazzaro calls, I think rightly, "one of the most horrifying
that Lowell has written."[24] There are two speakers, the
persona proper, who is male, and his dead wife, who
was insane. We end with the insane and utterly devout
wife urging her husband to "sit and listen" like "a red
cement Saint Francis":

So
I sat. I counted to ten thousand, wound
My cowhorn beads from Dublin on my thumb,
And ground them. *Miserere?* Not a sound.

And the poem's initial lines flow just as easily, just as
fully and richly:

Thanksgiving night: Third Avenue was dead,
My fowl was soupbones. Fathoms overhead,
Snow warred on the El's world in the blank snow.

The form of the poem, too, shows clear signs of relaxation.
Rather than stanzaic, it is written in what might better
be termed strophes, verse paragraphs that do not match
one another in length, in structure, or in rhyme patterns.
More important, perhaps, is the fact that the poem's
lines vary greatly in length, a strong indication that
formal processes have not been controlling in its com-

position, and a sign pointing forward to *Life Studies,* his next book. Even Lowell's insistent enjambments, often more trick than poetically valid in many of the earlier poems, here become wonderfully functional. " 'Let me go!/ Michael,' she whispered, 'all I want to do/ Is kill you'." This is by no means the only such example. My own favorite is a quite extraordinary feat of shock suspended, where it is precisely the enjambment which creates the effect, keeping the real thrust from us to the very last word: " 'But Michael, I was well;/ My mind was well;/ I wanted to be loved—to thaw, to change/ To *April!*' " (The italics are Lowell's.)

Technique, in short, is here wholly at the service of substance; Lowell seems to me to have tapped a deep vein, and a true one. Surely, if he had been able to continue down this road, he would have. He did not, and plainly he could not. Lowell could reach rich and consistent veins of poetry only—in a sense—by opening his own veins. That was a process he naturally did not relish; it turned out, too, to be a process he could not sustain. But let us now turn to Lowell's fourth and probably greatest book, *Life Studies,* published in 1959, where the veins were opened and the poetry flowed as never before or after.

3

Plugging into Life;
the Plug Refuses to Hold:
Life Studies and After

Lowell's first three books appeared over a period of seven years; his fourth, *Life Studies*, was published after an interval of eight years. So long a silence was not so much a sign of poetic struggle and uncertainty as it was the direct result of a thrashing and desperate search which, as I have said, persuaded some who knew him that he was written out. It might be more accurate, with the aid of hindsight, to say that he was written in, boxed in by borrowed attitudes and techniques that could no longer serve him and which, in my view, never did serve him. Lowell's comparative triumph in *Lord Weary's Castle* is in a sense a triumph over himself. And his almost total failure in *The Mills of the Kavanaughs* is in this same sense proof positive that he could no longer even partially succeed by flogging himself across obstacles he had put in his own way.

And Lowell's metrics, the musical organization of his verse, offer evidence of a different but no less certain sort. Although there are signs of a progressive loosening in the originally tight forms and metrical patterns of his poetry, from *Land of Unlikeness* to the short poems of *The Mills of the Kavanaughs*, until *Life Studies* appeared Lowell was a poet of traditional techniques and conservative, even at times reactionary, social stances. What M. L. Rosenthal has called "the revolutionary breakthrough of *Life Studies*,"[1] accordingly, necessarily comes

out of the interaction of many factors. But three such
factors seem to me primary: (1) his need for and push
toward self-knowledge, which for a poet usually means
self-revelation, had been present (but suppressed) from
the beginning, and had now grown too insistent, too
demanding, to be contained by conventional, restrictive
forms and meters; (2) his political and social beliefs and
actions had grown almost radical, thus bringing him into
association and often into alliance with Allen Ginsberg,
Norman Mailer, and many other "champions of one Left
cause or another"[2]; and (3) both political activity and
poetic need combined, as he read the poetry of Ginsberg
and others with newly opened eyes, to convince him
that a loose, free approach was in fact working for these
poetic and political radicals, was allowing them to make
use of the contemporary world in their art as he longed,
but had previously been unable, to do.

Nor do we need to simply speculate about Lowell's
changed procedures, or to try to deduce them from the
poetic texts of *Life Studies*. Lowell was too honest to
conceal either his concerns or his debts. Writing in 1964,
he explained how, in 1957, he had found what he needed:

I was in San Francisco, the era and setting of Allen Ginsberg
. . . I became sorely aware of how few poems I had written,
and that these few had been finished at the latest three or four
years earlier. Their style seemed distant, symbol-ridden and
wilfully difficult. I began to . . . add extra syllables to a line
to make it clearer and more colloquial. I felt my old poems hid
what they were really about, and many times offered a stiff,
humorless and even impenetrable surface. . . . My . . . poems
seemed like prehistoric monsters dragged down into the bog
and death by their ponderous armor. . . . I felt that the best
style for poetry was none of the many poetic styles in English,
but something like the prose of Chekhov or Flaubert. . . . I
felt that most of what I knew about writing was a hindrance.[3]

And in a 1961 interview he was even more explicit.
Reading his poems aloud, he explained, "I found that I

was simplifying [them]. If I had a Latin quotation I'd translate it into English. If adding a couple of syllables in a line made it clearer, I'd add them . . . very slight little changes, and I didn't change the printed text. It was just done for the moment." Asked if content had become more important, suddenly, than form, Lowell said, in essence, exactly so. "I began to have a certain disrespect for the tight forms. If you could make it easier by adding syllables, why not?"[4] He had moved, in short, a long step away from Allen Tate, and an even longer step away from Richard Eberhart (who was surely one of the very few to think *Lord Weary's Castle* inferior to *Land of Unlikeness*, and almost alone in approving of *The Mills of the Kavanaughs*). He had come a good deal closer, indeed, to the views of Ezra Pound, who spent his life insisting on "clarity and precision, upon the prose tradition; in brief, upon efficient writing—even in verse."[5] In the 1961 interview, significantly, Lowell observed that "prose is in many ways better off than poetry. . . . On the whole prose is less cut off from life than poetry is."[6]

Life Studies is of course neither an extended exercise in the writing of free verse, nor even a tightly unified, through-composed structure. It was written, and re-written, and pieced together over many years; some of the poems were first written in formal metrical and rhyme schemes and then irregularized; some were first written in prose.[7] And there are moments which remind us that Lowell is still struggling with the rhetorical frenzies of the earlier (and especially the earliest) verse. "I heard/ the El's green girders charge on Third," he writes in "Inauguration Day: January 1953," and then he slips briefly back into his old vice of clotted over-statement: "Manhattan's truss of adamant,/ that groaned in ermine, slummed on want." "A Mad Negro Soldier Confined at Munich," to be sure one of the earliest poems in the book, has six regular four-line stanzas,

closely rhymed, and definitely in the traditional iambic
pentameter metric. The last six lines of "For George
Santayana," on the whole unrhymed and certainly not
in any fixed metrical or structural pattern, break into so
determined a formal pattern, iambic pentameter metric
and close rhyming, that I suspect this was at one time
the closing portion of a formal Italian sonnet. The first
two lines of "Man and Wife" similarly form a perfectly
crafted heroic (end-stopped) iambic pentameter couplet:
"Tamed by *Miltown*, we lie on Mother's bed;/ the rising
sun in war paint dyes us red . . . " There is not much
rhyme in the rest of the poem and no discernible
traditional pattern. "To Speak of Woe That Is in Marriage," perhaps the worst poem in the book, is a slightly
irregular sonnet, rhymed however as couplets rather
than as more usual sonnets rhyme. And even the final
poem, "Skunk Hour," arguably the finest thing Lowell
ever wrote, is composed in eight stanzas of six lines each;
the stanzas have irregular line lengths, and the rhyming
too is irregular, but every stanza has recognizable
rhymes, and the final stanza is fully rhymed.

The book has four parts: the first is the shortest, as
well as the earliest to be written, and features only four
short poems; the second is a prose memoir; the third is
again short and again has only four poems, each with a
dead writer as its commemorative subject; and the
fourth, subtitled "Life Studies" and subdivided into two
sections, is both the longest and the most important. I
want to briefly discuss the two shortest sections, parts
one and three, and to briefly comment on the prose
memoir; the final and most important part ought to and
will receive the fullest discussion.

The best of the four poems in part one is also the
first in that section, "Beyond the Alps." Tricked out with
what seems to be a pious epigraph, the poem might lead
us to expect the "twisting and disgust" (Lowell's own
phrase) of his first book. But we are immediately and

happily made aware that religion is no longer dogma, no longer some all-pervading pillar to which the poet desperately clings, praying loudly for support and comfort. He can be relaxed, now, he can be ironic, he can be everyday and conversational and real:

> Reading how even the Swiss had thrown the sponge
> in once again and Everest was still
> unscaled, I watched our Paris pullman lunge
> mooning across the fallow Alpine snow.
> *O bella Roma!* I saw our stewards go
> forward on tiptoe banging on their gongs.
> Life changed to landscape. Much against my will
> I left the City of God where it belongs.

Still in a slightly loosened iambic pentameter, and very freely and unconventionally rhymed, this is nevertheless lighter in tone, more relaxed in movement than anything in the first three volumes of his poetry. "Thrown the sponge/ in" is not only slangy but fits extremely well with the pullman car lunging across the snow. And the poet seems to intend that we carry the jocular, faintly ludicrous image from one setting to the other. His use of a phrase in Italian strikes me, here, as deeply comic. And he does not simply toss it in and leave it, but follows it with a piece of chinoiserie that might have come out of a Gilbert and Sullivan operetta: "I saw our stewards go/ forward on tiptoe banging on their gongs." The train moves, the people disappear ("Life changed to landscape"), and the onetime mouth-foaming convert to Catholicism can say of Rome, now, that he has left it "where it belongs."

After some fine, easy parading of "our grandparents on their grand tours—/ long-haired Victorian sages accept[ing] the universe,/ while breezing on their trust funds through the world," and some eminently sensible, eminently reasonable and relaxed talk of the Pope and his new dogma ("But who believed this? Who could understand?"), we are brought to an extended metaphor

founded in classical Greek poetry, but here fully prepared
for, fully relevant, not intrusively laid on like thick slabs
of elegant but imported marble. When dawn is observed
in the high Alps, dawn is perfectly legitimately presented
as "Apollo plant[ing] his heels/ on terra firma through
the morning's thigh." Each "wasted Alp" is deftly anal-
ogized to the wasted Parthenon, but we are also reminded
that physical elevation does not necessarily equate with
moral and literary altitude: "There were no tickets for
that altitude/ once held by Hellas . . . " And the final
two lines, set off as the rhymed couplet they are, follow
from, and are developed out of, this extended Greek
material: "Now Paris, our black classic, breaking up/ like
killer kings on an Etruscan cup." The great, dirty
metropolis is in fact black, and so too are Etruscan cups,
which frequently have killer kings painted onto them.
But the Etruscans were also the predecessors of the
Latin peoples in possession of Rome: we may have "left
the City of God where it belongs," but it is not some
solipsist's vision that disappears when we leave it. Rome
endures, and requires that we deal with it—which makes
still more powerful and meaningful Lowell's delicate,
rather mocking description of the doctrine of Mary's
bodily Assumption, earlier in the poem. And it helps
transform what might have been no more than a clever
travel poem into a deeply moving meditation. (It is also
worth noting, though perhaps only poets fully appreciate
the importance of such small matters, that this and all
the poems in the book now capitalize the first word in
a line only when it is also the first word of a sentence.
It is an additional small break with tradition and a
significant aid in the general lightening of both tone and
verse movement.)

Lowell's prose memoir, forming part two of the
book, needs no detailed commentary—it speaks extremely well for itself. Whether each and every autobiographical detail is or is not accurate—most are—is a

good deal less important than the overall weight and direction given to the poetry by this crisp, dismal, and probably purgative prose. Poets often write prose poems and include them in their books of poetry; poets write prose, too, and publish it—fiction and criticism and autobiography. But a mixture of poems and a long prose memoir was virtually unknown before *Life Studies*, and even in the over two decades since its publication has not been common. The mixture, bluntly, is extremely hard to sustain, esthetically: either poems or prose tend to outweigh one another. A book of this nature is not the place to attempt an analysis, but it seems plain that Lowell has managed to key poems and prose to each other—to scale the poetic rhetoric toward prose, and to elevate the prose tone toward poetry—and at the same time to catch enough of his own voice, in both forms, so that the reader feels no shock when moving from one to the other. It is a feat worth celebrating, and one exceedingly difficult to imitate. And simply as an act of delicate and subtle balance, it further indicates the artistic control Lowell can now wield: in many ways it is the sheer *authority* of his writing, in *Life Studies*, which makes it so impressive, enduring, and affecting a book. Balance, as I noted earlier, is virtually the last characteristic we might expect from the author of *Land of Unlikeness*.

Each of the four poems in part three is I think an unqualified success—and how often, in regard to the earlier volumes, has any critic, no matter how friendly, been able to wax so enthusiastic? Again, I want to focus exclusively on the most powerful among these poems, "To Delmore Schwartz." And I also want to highlight the metrical nature of the poem, since as I have said the prosody of *Life Studies* is part and parcel both of its "revolutionary" nature and its great achievement. There are plain irregularities in the poems to Ford Madox Ford and to George Santayana (though not in the short "Words

for Hart Crane," which is yet again a structurally irregular
sonnet—that form of all forms toward which, in the end,
Lowell gravitated). But it is in the Delmore Schwartz
poem, the best of the four, that prosodic irregularities
accumulate to the point where, had it been set in a group
of free verse poems, it would not have been out of place.
It rhymes, but in no pattern whatever, and sometimes
across so many intervening lines that the eye can scarcely
pick it up and the ear simply cannot hear it. Here, then,
is the first strophe, introducing us to the two young
poets ("Cambridge 1946" is the subtitle), who over the
years proved to be more alike than either of them knew
at the time. And it is worth emphasizing that, while
Schwartz was Jewish and Lowell came from a long long
line of Puritans and was soon to convert to Catholicism,
the prose memoir of *Life Studies* has occupied its first
three pages with an account of Lowell's one Jewish
ancestor, Major Mordecai Meyers.

> We couldn't even keep the furnace lit!
> Even when we had disconnected it
> the antiquated
> refrigerator gurgled mustard gas
> through your mustard-yellow house
> and spoiled our long maneuvered visit
> from T. S. Eliot's brother, Henry Ware. . . .

Pretty clearly, iambic pentameter is the metre that the
poem avoids (though lines 1, 2, 4, and 7 can be scanned
as iambic pentameter), and even when more or less
employing it Lowell stretches it badly, as in line 2,
probably to be read "EVen WHEN we had DIScon-
NECted IT," a pretty bumpy line for a traditional poem.
"Visit" is a "feeble" rhyme (*rime faible*) for the regular
"lit/it" rhyme of lines 1 and 2; "antiquated" in line 3
obviously rhymes with nothing; and if "gas" in line 4
rhymes at all with "house" in line 5 it is at best
exceedingly attenuated. And "Ware" in line 7 does not
rhyme with anything: though nine full lines farther along

a line ends with "stare," it is immediately followed by
the end- and rhyme-word, "there," suggesting clearly
that even Lowell did not think a rhyme could possibly
arc across so vast a poetic space.

Note that both the shared events described and the
language used to describe those events—"we" is repeated
insistently, and for all the personal, subjective aura there
is not a single "I" anywhere in the poem—are insistently
focussed on the here-and-now, the immediate world.
And the poem radiates the joy of that sharing: again, joy
has not been an easy thing to find in Lowell's earlier
volumes.

> Your stuffed duck craned toward Harvard from my trunk;
> its bill was a black whistle, and its brow
> was high and thinner than a baby's thumb;
> its webs were tough as toenails on its bough.

This part whimsical, part good-humoredly self-mocking
passage would have been smothered, had it even been
attempted, in the earlier books. One cannot pile arcane
allusions and portentousness of any sort on a "stuffed
duck." Indeed, though I cannot quote the entire sequence, Delmore Schwartz's toy animal gets no less than
thirteen full lines, and they are wonderfully consistent,
consecutive, interwoven as never before in Lowell's
poetry. There seems to be no need, now, to draw on
material outside of the poet's immediate experience, to
rely on external things to prop up what cannot quite
stand on its own. His metaphors too evolve naturally
from these facts of immediate experience. The toy duck's
"high brow" is "thinner than a baby's thumb"—and is
perhaps also a nicely, neatly concealed pun on the
highbrow young poets themselves. The duck's webs are
"tough as toenails." So deft a fusion of *things* and theme
is, as Lowell's earlier books all prove, one of the hardest
masteries to obtain.

> "Let Joyce and Freud,
>   the Masters of Joy,

be our guests here," you said. The room was filled
with cigarette smoke circling the paranoid,
inert gaze of Coleridge, back
from Malta—his eyes lost in flesh, lips baked and black.

The joyous punning on "joy," founded in the names of
the great Irish writer James Joyce and the great Viennese
master of psychiatry, whose name means "joy" in German, leads into a lightly handled but deeply serious
evocation of that archetypical poetic failure, Coleridge.
Virtually all artists worry about failure, and even after
his enormous early successes in the 1930s Delmore
Schwartz worried about it with steadily growing paranoia;
he drove himself into an artistic, and then a personal,
decline that ended with his death in 1966 in a shabby
rooming house, alone and almost forgotten.[8] But again
showing a fine and delicate balance, Lowell does not
dwell on the "paranoid,/ inert" Coleridge. "Your tiger
kitten, *Oranges,*/ cartwheeled for joy in a ball of snarls."
It is only two lines, and then we are taken back to the
world of poets and poetry, but the easing is marked and
important. Note too how deftly Lowell moves from the
puppyish joy of the two poets to the kittenish joy of the
little cat. And then, as I said, back to serious matters—
but not desperately serious:

You said:
"We poets in our youth begin in sadness;
thereof in the end come despondency and madness;
Stalin has had two cerebral hemorrhages!"
The Charles
River was turning silver. In the ebb-
light of morning, we stuck
the duck
-'s web-
foot, like a candle, in a quart of gin we'd killed.

These are the final lines of the poem, taking us from the
good-humored whimsy of the opening lines to this
nostalgic and yet distinctly lyric affirmation. It seems to
me typical of Lowell's newfound assurance that he can

permit himself the romantic tinge of "The Charles/ River was turning silver." It is also demonstrative of his newfound power that he can so smoothly blend his image of the river silvered by predawn light with the infinitely less traditional image of the stuffed duck's foot jammed, "like a candle, in a quart of gin." And it is also a singularly beautiful way of fusing the two divergent notions, namely river water and light: plainly, it is primarily water that ebbs, and not light.

The unusual line breaks (unusual, that is, for Lowell: poets like e. e. cummings and others had been using more unusual ones for many years) probably conceal the metrical irregularities of the final three lines. "The DUCK'S WEB-FOOT, like a CANdle, in a QUART . . . ," which scans as I have here marked it, is neither iambic nor any other traditional metrical pattern. Further, Lowell has so placed the penultimate line, "-'s web-," that it is hard *not* to stress it, producing what might be called a triple spondee, that is, three stresses in a row, with no intervening unstressed syllables. It is I believe the first such metrical anomaly in all of Lowell's work. Indeed, his final rhyme-word, "killed," is both a weak rhyme, since the other half of the pairing is "silver" four lines earlier, and is also slant- rather than end-rhyme—that is, "silver" is not the final word in the line.

And on all levels, technical and substantive alike, I think we have finally arrived, with this poem, at what seems to be that immensely satisfying moment when a potentially great poet becomes, at least in some ways, actually great and begins to write at least some unequivocally great poetry. Anyone who has followed, or who has traced after-the-fact, the career of a great poet, can recognize here what would seem to be the sure signs. The whole process seems almost inevitable, almost predictable.

But Robert Lowell was I'm afraid simply not like other poets of major stature; he is not predictable at any stage of his career, and none of his turnings—or indeed his nonturnings—seem to me, in truth, inevitable. And though it is easy enough, here, to sense Lowell poised—finally—for that full-scale storming up the last and highest slopes of Mount Olympus, toward which final ascent most poets, and most artists generally, strive and struggle for years, it must bluntly be said, with both regret and some bewilderment, that it just does not happen. To put it differently, for whatever reason Lowell would not allow it to happen—until, that is, he was within days of his death.

Part four of *Life Studies* is a considerable achievement, containing perhaps the best of all Lowell's poems, "Skunk Hour." But in most of this section, as in all but one of the books of verse which come after it, I see, not further consolidation and higher accomplishment, but a falling off, a renewed and in the end a deepening and apparently almost permanent failure of nerve. It is a falling off, however, only in the sense that Lowell does not, in my judgment, move onto the extraordinarily high ground which "To Delmore Schwartz" and "Skunk Hour" indicate he was entitled to occupy, and for which his distinctive and compelling magic of expression, his unique and appealing poetic voice, would seem to have made him inevitably destined. Everything was present, that is, except the willingness to make full use of his newfound balance, his newfound ease, and the powers that had been his all along. Having gained the foothills of Olympus, in a sense, by a stunning march into what had been the enemy camp, having learned how to gear down his hyperactive poetic machine, it was only at the very end of his life that Lowell was able, somehow, to speed it back up again. Until that terribly final volume, almost a deathbed production—*Day by Day*, to be discussed in chapter four—there is I think nothing after *Life Studies*, not a single complete poem in any of the books he poured into print, that reaches the level of the two poems just discussed. In a different context, Lowell himself said, in a 1968 interview, "I no longer know the difference between prose and verse."[9] And that damaging inability is, I think, already clear in almost all the poems of this fourth and last part, subtitled "Life Studies."

> "I won't go with you. I want to stay with Grandpa!"
> That's how I threw cold water
> on my Mother and Father's
> watery martini pipe dreams at Sunday dinner.

This is the opening of the four-part poem, "My Last Afternoon with Uncle Devereux Winslow," which leads off part four of the book. This is easy, deft verse, with a good sense of openness and a nice forward movement. It is consistent, it is appealing: "cold water," in line 2, neatly prepares us for the "watery pipe dreams" of line 4, and indeed all the props, all the detail and image material, are perfectly appropriate to both the poem and to its approach. But this easy-flowing, virtuosic poetry does not dig very deep—what we see, here and hereafter, is what we get. It is a splendidly worked surface, one that most poets are incapable of creating, but it is emphatically not great poetry by any definition that makes sense to me. It makes good reading; it is often fun; it is sometimes touching; and it is always appealing—and these are by no means qualities to be despised. But, for all that, it simply does not add up to either the stature Lowell seemed to have achieved nor to that which has been so often claimed for him.

> Our farmer was cementing a root-house under the hill.
> One of my hands was cool on a pile
> of black earth, the other warm
> on a pile of lime. All about me
> were the works of my Grandfather's hands:
> snapshots of his *Liberty Bell* silver mine;
> his high school at *Stukkert am Neckar;*
> stogie-brown beams; fool's-gold nuggets;
> octagonal red tiles,
> sweaty with a secret dank, crummy with ant-stale;

a Rocky Mountain chaise longue,
its legs, shellacked saplings.
A pastel-pale Huckleberry Finn
fished with a broom straw in a basin
hollowed out of a millstone.
Like my Grandfather, the décor
was manly, comfortable,
overbearing, disproportioned.

This long passage occurs some fifteen lines after the
opening lines I have quoted; and it seems to me
essentially no different. And though there are felicities,
sometimes delightful felicities, scattered all across the
poem, choicely phrased lines within the reach of very
few poets, we are engaged only in a limited way. This
is immensely attractive poetry; it is distinctly successful
in what it tries to do. But it does not try to do very
much, and certainly not much in comparison to what
Lowell has shown, elsewhere in *Life Studies*, that he
can do.

One such poem of larger aim is "Man and Wife,"
from the second subdivision of this fourth part of the
book. It opens in a masterfully controlled passage, as
stately as anything written by Alexander Pope (and not
unlike Pope in formal matters: the first four lines in
particular are perfect Popean heroic, end-stopped couplets):

Tamed by *Miltown*, we lie on Mother's bed;
the rising sun in war paint dyes us red;
in broad daylight her gilded bed-posts shine,
abandoned, almost Dionysian.
At last the trees are green on Marlborough Street,
blossoms on our magnolia ignite
the morning with their murderous five days' white.

The truly fierce intensity of lines 6 and 7 is heightened
by that Popean stateliness. It is a substantive formality
he has invoked, here, and yet further proof of his
technical mastery. "The rising sun in war paint" might

have been an isolated stroke, a brilliant but not a fully functioning image, even as late as *Lord Weary's Castle*. Here, however, not only does it immediately carry us into, and illuminate, "dyes us red," it also prepares us for the beautiful and terrible gleam of the magnolia blossoms, their "five days' white" stunningly presented to us as "murderous." And Lowell does not drop off from this stark beginning; there is no failure of nerve in this poem. "All night I've held your hand," he continues at once, leading us into a tightly woven, compressed reprise of his and his second wife's early years together. The bare final lines, accordingly, are deeply moving:

> Now twelve years later, you turn your back.
> Sleepless, you hold
> your pillow to your hollows like a child;
> your old-fashioned tirade—
> loving, rapid, merciless—
> breaks like the Atlantic Ocean on my head.

The greatness of the poem, it seems to me, lies in the blunt power with which Lowell has dealt with his own ambivalence in this tense and difficult relationship. He has described her, in a passage I have not quoted, as "my *Petite*,/ clearest of all God's creatures, still all air and nerve," surely a portrait of someone who simultaneously attracts and irritates, even repels, him. In the passage just quoted, which concludes the poem, to say of her that she holds her "pillow to [her] hollows like a child" is equally ambivalent. It would be different were she in fact a child; she is in fact plainly not. And the "old-fashioned" tirade is similarly two-edged. "Old-fashioned" is probably positive, though perhaps not completely so; "tirade" may indicate tolerance, here, but it also indicates resentment and hostility. And even the three final adjectives of the penultimate line—"loving, rapid, merciless"—continue the pattern of painful, deeply unsentimentalized honesty. "Loving" is of course totally positive; "rapid" is somewhat less positive, though

not necessarily negative; "merciless," if it is to be
understood as praise, is at best extremely uncomfortable
praise. Again, it is the poet's courage, his capacity to
face, and in a sense perhaps even to face down, himself
that enables the poem to be so charged, so taut, just as
it is his comparative lack of courage which leaves the
bulk of these poems, good as they are, in the final
analysis rather slack. In the next chapter, indeed, I will
call the bulk of his poetry after *Near the Ocean* a kind
of distinguished poetic journalism—and the phrase will
be intended quite as ambivalently as was "Man and
Wife."[10]

"Skunk Hour" has received as much critical attention, I suspect, as any poem by a twentieth-century
American poet, with the possible exception of T. S.
Eliot's *The Waste Land*. There are fine essays by both
Lowell's close friend, the American poet John Berryman,
and by Lowell himself, in the Parkinson collection of
essays about Lowell;[11] there are good discussions of the
poem by other poets, including Richard Wilbur and
John F. Nims;[12] most recently there is a fine discussion
by Richard J. Fein.[13] Every book on Lowell is obliged
to tackle the poem and, within limitations, this book
cannot be any exception, though the abundance of prior
commentary leads me to deal with the poem as briefly
as possible.

Although he added another poem in the paperback
edition of *Life Studies*, and gave it the final and weightiest
place in that edition, Lowell's original scheme carefully
set "Skunk Hour" at the very end of the book.[14] Once
titled, in an earlier draft, "Inspiration," the poem is only
forty-eight lines long. Lowell has himself called it "the
dark night," invoking San Juan de la Cruz's great poem
of torment and yet of faith, "The Dark Night of the
Soul." But that is intention and background. What
emerges on the page is a savage attack on both the
capitalist society in which we Americans live and the

sort of spiritual/human isolation in which that society can lock us up. Set in a Maine vacation resort, the poem spends two stanzas on the senile heiress who, wishing she were safely back in "Queen Victoria's century, . . . buys up all/ the eyesores facing her shore,/ and lets them fall." It moves to "our summer millionaire," one of the nouveau riche "who seemed to leap from an L. L. Bean [an expensive mail-order shop]/ catalogue," but has apparently gone bankrupt: "His nine-yacht yawl/ was auctioned off to lobstermen." The fourth stanza takes out after a homosexual shopkeeper who'd "rather marry"—and specifically because "there is no money in his work." In short, this first half of the poem gives us the social setting, but that social setting is seen almost overwhelming in fiscal terms. The dotty old lady has money and therefore power; the "summer millionaire" had money and had power and now has nothing; the "fairy/decorator" works, but in fiscal terms at least wanes rather than waxes.

Two things seem to me primary about these opening twenty-four lines. First, they are singularly sparse, even hard; there is not the slightest sentimentality, nor is there any apparent exaggeration. This is the world of Nautilus Island as Lowell in fact sees it. He paints that world with devastating abruptness. And second, and just as important, this scene-setting is then used, applied— and deepened—in what follows. Starting in stanza five, the poem says not a word more about dotty heiress, fallen millionaire, or scrabbling homosexual. The background firmly in place, Lowell introduces his main character, who is not surprisingly himself. He drives to the local lover's lane, trying—if even at secondhand—to experience some fragmentary sense of love and closeness to another human being. "My mind's not right," he tells us, but though we are given no reason to doubt that statement, neither can we escape the impact of the poem's first four stanzas. That is, the persona of the

poem is mad against the background so harshly drawn
in: even the "love-cars" he drives up the hill to watch
are described to us as lying "together, hull to hull,/
where the graveyard shelves on the town." The individual
neither does nor can escape the society he emerges both
into and out of, as the lovers in their parked cars cannot
escape the graveyard alongside them. Hearing a haunting
love song from one of the car radios the persona cries,
silently and to himself, that "I myself am hell;/ nobody's
here." The deep split between society and the individual
is perfectly captured in these two short lines. On the
one hand he is, as we all are, his own hell. On the other
hand, salvation and succor are withheld precisely because
he is alone, precisely because he has no one to give him
what he needs.

   And yet, that help is in fact there—for, despite the
lack of contact with the lovers in their cars, determinedly
(and properly) oblivious of him, the persona is not alone,
and the line "nobody's here" does not end with a period,
but with a dramatic dash, indicative of more to come.
And though what comes is in fact "only skunks," the
persona—now no longer in his car and on the hill, but
on "our back steps"—can see that courage, that rarest
of all traits, is displayed by animals as well as humans,
and spells one visibly possible road to salvation—for him
as well as for the skunks. Here is the final stanza:

> I stand on top
> of our back steps and breathe the rich air—
> a mother skunk with her column of kittens swills the
>   garbage pail.
> She jabs her wedge-head in a cup
> of sour cream, drops her ostrich tail,
> and will not scare.

It would be hard, I think, to overpraise such writing as
this. Lowell is so tightly in control, indeed, that he can—
with a show of casualness lesser poets can only gape at—
toss in a grim yet also a comic joke. The air, plainly, is

"rich" primarily because the skunks have disturbed the garbage: bluntly, it stinks. And yet there is also the sense that another sort of richness is also evident, the survival-determination of these small animals, confronted with but not overcome by exactly the same society of humans faced by the persona. "Back steps" is a carefully homely phrase. Heroes do not stand on back steps, and noble deeds are not there performed. On the other hand, "breathe" is not exactly what we expect. Standing "on top" of back steps, even the persona of a poem is somehow more likely to reach, to stretch, to bend, than simply to stand and do nothing. The uncertainty of just what is "rich" is thus compounded, and then trebled, for Lowell deliberately paints the mother skunk to almost heroic proportions, her physical beauty being equated to that of a much larger creature, namely the ostrich, and her immense courage being stated in the flattest of terms: she "will not scare." In just this one stanza, in short, Lowell has pushed and pulled us from one stance to another, realization partially canceling out realization, until we cannot at the end say with absolute certainty just what we have undergone. But we do know that it has been intense, and we know the main outlines of it, and we leave the poem with renewed hope for ourselves, too, as well as for the persona. And we leave it— inescapably, it seems to me—stirred as deeply as one can be stirred. And no work of art accomplishes such things by thematic means alone. This is magnificent poetry, and it is written magnificently, with enormous craft, utilizing immense resources of both technique and feeling.

But, once again, Lowell could not keep it up.

Published five years later, in 1964, *For the Union Dead* is not a bad book so much as a tired one. It has some fine passages, but it does not contain a single finished poem of first-rate accomplishment. Even Helen

Vendler, a superb critic who I think at times overpraises
Lowell, calls *For the Union Dead* and the book that
followed it three years later, *Near the Ocean*, "Lowell's
two weaker volumes," warning us "that Lowell had to
find a new impulse of energy or die as a poet."[15] And
that sense of groping, and not finding, dominates the
book from start to finish.

For example, "Water," the very first poem, is visibly
shaded toward what Lowell hopes will become a new
sort of lyric form, an easier, more open structure which
might more readily match and more comfortably contain
the new more flowing verse he had been writing.

> It was a Maine lobster town—
> each morning boatloads of hands
> pushed off for granite
> quarries on the islands,
>
> and left dozens of bleak
> white frame houses stuck
> like oyster shells
> on a hill of rock . . .

The obvious model for this unfortunately rather slack
poetry is William Carlos Williams.[16] But Lowell achieves
neither the lyricism nor the compressed intensity of
Williams, settling rather for something not much more
musical than good evocative prose. One major key to
Lowell's comparative failure, here, is his lineation. Line
breaks occur for no particularly important reason; the
stanzas can be rearranged without any loss (or any gain):

> It was a Maine lobster town—
> each morning boatloads of hands pushed off
> for granite quarries
> on the islands . . .

So too, in "The Old Flame," which ends with man
and wife, in marital discord, hearing a snow plow
"groaning up hill—/ a red light, then a blue,/ as it tossed

off the snow/to the side of the road," the description is
so neutral, so little the image or the symbol the poet
seems to think it, that details can be added or subtracted
without either loss or gain. Consider instead a plow
"pushing up hill—/ a blue light, then a white,/ while it
piled up the snow/ all alongside the road." In the same
poem Lowell writes "Everything's changed for the best—
/ how quivering and fierce we were . . . " and we know,
alas, that he has said all he means or perhaps is able to
say. Bluntly, the lines just quoted seem to me more
appropriate to a letter, or even to a conversational
exchange, than to a poem. There is a difference between
poetic terseness and prosaic flatness, and Lowell—as he
himself also recognized; recall his already quoted obser-
vation that "I no longer know the difference between
prose and verse"—seems unable to establish that difference. The first stanza of the next poem, "Middle Age,"
demonstrates this incapacity vividly: "Now the midwinter
grind/ is on me, New York/ drills through my nerves,/
as I walk/ the chewed-up streets." "The midwinter grind"
is very nearly a prose cliché; walking "the chewed-up
streets" is straight but unexceptional prose; and the
attempted metaphor, the city drilling "through my
nerves," is embarrassingly stale.

This same poem also shows a different sort of flailing
about, namely the use of unnecessary repetitions in
order to give a more "poetic" flavor: "At forty-five,/ what
next, what next?" Such mechanical writing, to which
Lowell adds an excessive use of exclamation marks and
a heavy reliance on expletives like "Oh" and "Ah," gives
much of the book an oddly amateurish flavor. In "The
Scream," he tries to somewhat vary this tired, mechanistic verse, but comes up largely empty-handed: "Back
and away and back!/ Mother kept coming and going—/
with me, without me!/ Mother's dresses were black/ or
white, or black-and-white." This poem describes "cow
flop" as sounding *"smack, smack, smack!"*, just as, in

"Fall 1961," we are told that the grandfather clock goes "tock, tock, tock . . . " and by the end that it goes "Back and forth!/ Back and forth, back and forth . . . " "Oh Florence, Florence," he wails in the poem entitled "Florence," and a few lines further on simply repeats an entire line: "Pity the monsters!/ Pity the monsters!" There is a similar straining after gnats, throughout the book, in his distinctly mechanical wordplay. "We are where we were," he asserts in "The Lesson," and immediately reasserts, as if actually adding to the original statement, "We were!" In "Those Before Us," he does almost the same thing, first saying "they play/ their thankless, fill-in roles," then adding that "They never were." Even the soundplay gets mechanistic and rather desperate-seeming: "I dabble in the dapple of the day," he writes in "Night Sweat," having just a few lines earlier told us that "I feel the light/ lighten . . . " In a thoroughly awful travel and social-consciousness poem, "Dropping South: Brazil," he even descends to the level of bad prose propaganda: "while inland, people starved, and struck, and died . . . " How whirled about in uncertainty must a great poet be, indeed, to tell us, in the poem "Buenos Aires," of "my sharp shoes/ that hurt my toes." And how exceedingly desperate to exclaim in "The Neo-Classical Urn": "Oh neo-classical white urn, Oh nymph,/ Oh lute!"

And yet, though I have not exhausted (and will not try to exhaust) the catalogue of failures, there are passages throughout the book that are as electrifyingly powerful as anything written in this century. "Florence," for example, which descends to the bathos of "Ah, to have known, to have loved/ too many Davids and Judiths!" begins with this majestic and magnificent strophe:

> I long for the black ink,
> cuttlefish, April, Communists
> and brothels of Florence—
> everything, even the British

fairies who haunted the hills,
even the chills and fever
that came once a month
and forced me to think.
The apple was more human there than here,
but it took a long time for the blinding
golden rind to mellow.

"Middle Age" begins very badly, and does not get any better until the final stanza, which in a sense points to the poem about his dead father that he might have written, but could not write: "You never climbed/ Mount Sion, yet left/ dinosaur/ death-steps on the crust,/ where I must walk." A heavily padded poem, "Eye and Tooth," has stanzas that, had they been built into a full-scale and viable structure, might have been breathtaking: "I lay all day on my bed./ I chain-smoked through the night,/ learning to flinch/ at the flash of the matchlight." The last lines, indeed, might be an epigraph for the entire book: "No oil/ for the eye, nothing to pour/ on those waters or flames./ I am tired. Everyone's tired of my turmoil."

Two poems approach, though they do not reach, consistent effectiveness. One is "The Public Garden," reworked and much improved from his long failure, "The Mills of the Kavanaughs." The garden is "burned-out" in the first line; we are assured that "Nothing catches fire" in the last line; and the sense of a relatively unified structure is more or less carried out through the whole poem, though there is padding and there is some rather sideways movement. But there is also some of that riveting Lowell vision which, to my mind, no other poet of our time has matched. "Dead leaves thicken to a ball/ inside the basin of a fountain," one such passage begins, mildly enough, and then the power is turned on: " . . . where/ the heads of four stone lions stare/ and suck on empty fawcets." It is the two verbs, "stare" and "suck," that carry the voltage—and the voltage is immense. Later in the poem, after a nice but hardly electrifying bit about the moon, which "lies like chalk/ over the waters," Lowell first sums up, pleasantly, in a short statement: "Everything's aground." And then he turns, and the poem pivots with him, in what seems to me one of the most beautiful brief apostrophes in our literature: "Remember summer?" The aching contrast, which ties in well with the "burned-out" mood of the poem, strikes like a cobra.[17]

"For the Union Dead," clearly the best poem in the book, seems almost to harken back to the methods and the style of *Lord Weary's Castle*.[18] Written around, though not strictly about, the Boston statue commemorating young Colonel Robert Gould Shaw, who led the black soldiers under his command in an almost suicidal charge on a Confederate fort and, along with many of his men, was killed, the poem is prefaced with the Latin inscription placed on that statue (and composed by Harvard's then president, Charles W. Eliot), which translated reads: "He leaves all to serve the state." Lowell's approach is, inevitably, both satiric and commemorative; the contrast between Shaw's straightforward heroism and the Boston of the 1960s is the poem's plain thrust. The "monument sticks like a fishbone/ in the city's throat," he tells us. "Its Colonel is as lean/ as a compass-needle." In contrast, the poem ends with "giant finned cars nos[ing] forward like fish," and the harsh condemnation of American society in the final lines, "a savage servility/ slides by on grease." And yet it seems to me a mistake to call the poem, as for example Axelrod does, "a seamless verbal fabric."[19] For all its excellences, it exhibits much the same slackness, the same sideways movement, the same sense of rather febrile padding as does the rest of the volume. In the description of the boarded-up old South Boston Aquarium with which the poem opens, only the first of the three stanzas devoted to that now-vanished institution are truly functional. We have been told all we need to know once we are shown the old building standing "in a Sahara of snow": "The bronze weathervane cod has lost half its scales./ The airy tanks are dry." But Lowell goes on, and much too long, about himself as a child, visiting the aquarium, when "my hand tingled/ to burst the bubbles/ drifting from the noses of the cowed, compliant fish." The push of the poem has been lost, here; Lowell-as-child has not been placed in the poem's structure, and to ramble on in this way is to seriously weaken a focus that lies elsewhere. But Lowell has still not done: "I often sigh still/ for the dark downward and vegetating kingdom/ of the fish and reptile," he tells us, and this is doubly out of focus. That is, not only does it stray from the then-now theme, but it starts to move, sideways as it were, toward a poem that Lowell is not here going to write, a poem about (perhaps) his sense of the relations of human and animal kingdoms, or about his personal sense of loss as he is faced with the visible destruction of the past. And before he can get us to Colonel Shaw and his statue, Lowell sweats through rather strained, contorted lines about "yellow dinosaur steamshovels" and "a girdle of orange, Puritan-pumpkin colored girders."

And, on the other hand, the poem moves from *Lord Weary's Castle* febrility to prosy, tired slackness. "Two months after marching through Boston,/half the regiment was dead;/ at the dedication,/ William James could almost hear the bronze Negroes breathe." The poetic journalism of part of *Life Studies* reappears, too: "On a thousand small town New England greens,/ the old white churches hold their air/ of sparse, sincere rebellion; frayed flags/ quilt the graveyards of the Grand Army of the Republic." This is pleasant, it is accurate, but it has no staying power; it does not reach beyond the neat surface. "Shaw's father," we are told, "wanted no monument/ except the ditch,/ where his son's body was thrown/ and lost with

his 'niggers'," and in what way are these lines much
more than clean prose? They report; they do not stir,
they do not sing. When Lowell tries to raise the pitch,
he strains: "When I crouch to my television set,/ the
drained faces of Negro school-children rise like balloons."
The sentiments are admirable; the poetry, for the last
time, is slack, weary, and not very convincing.

Near the Ocean, published in 1967, comes close to
being, as I said in chapter one, not a book of original
poetry at all. (It is also decorated with some of the most
inept line drawings I have even seen; I do not know
whether Lowell or his publishers are responsible for this
feeble artwork, produced by Sidney Nolan, but in other
Lowell volumes there is almost equally inept illustration
provided by one of Lowell's old schoolmates, Frank
Parker.) The great bulk of *Near the Ocean* consists of
imitations from Horace, Juvenal, Dante, and a fusion of
Quevedo and Góngora. The discussion of Lowell's *Imitations* volume in chapter five will deal with my approach
to his poems derived from work in other languages, to
which discussion these later imitations add little or
nothing. There are seven original poems in *Near the
Ocean*, ranging from the short, T. S. Eliot-influenced
"1958," which is yet another sonnet variant, to a series
of poems in an irregular eight-line stanza form of Lowell's
own devising, including the padded and slack "Central
Park" and a sixteen-line poem in memoriam Theodore
Roethke, which concludes with perhaps the most elegant
verse in the volume. Lowell assures the dead poet, his
friend, that

> Now, you honor the mother.
> Omnipresent,
> she made you nonexistent,
> the ocean's anchor, our high tide.

There are two problems with "For Theodore

Roethke," however, and once again they are represent-
ative of the book's problems as well. The first twelve
lines flounder, much as we saw the poems of *For the
Union Dead* floundering, trying to thrash their way into
the clear. "All night you wallowed through my sleep,"
the poem begins, "then in the morning you were lost/
in the Maine sky." The two key notions are (1) that the
memory of his dead poet-friend "wallowed" in his head,
as he slept, and (2) that in the morning even that memory
was "lost/in the . . . sky." But these are both, I'm afraid,
secondhand notions, the second of them, indeed, distinctly close to a clichéd notion. Trying to make the
second notion more like something truly alive, Lowell
adds, putting a dash after the word "sky—close, cold
and gray,/ smoke and smoke-colored cloud." These are
well-chosen words for the Maine sky, but they do nothing
for a memorial poem. That is, they do not fit with
Roethke or with any other dead poet; they do not fit
with grief or with remembrance; they have no focus,
they are merely descriptive. And competent description
is the bare beginning of poetry, not the finished product.
To say of Roethke, as Lowell does farther on, that "You
honored nature," is to say something so bland and
generalized that it means remarkably little, and moves
the reader hardly at all. To add, ambiguously, that nature
(or Roethke?) is a "helpless, elemental creature" is,
again, to say virtually nothing at all. The terms are too
vague, too unfocussed, to guide us, to move us. So too
the three lines earlier in the poem about a pair of "loons
devolving to a monochrome," might as well be printed
on a Maine picture postcard, for all the connection they
have, or are made to have, with either Lowell or
Roethke.

The second difficulty is, in a way, even more
damning. The high formalist tone of the last stanza of
the poem, though elegant and plainly very controlled,
is not recognizable as any tone belonging to Robert

Lowell. That is, in a word, Lowell has achieved this bit of elegance basically by derivation, by borrowing. We do not expect to see it continued or developed elsewhere in his poetry—and it is not. Lowell's elegance, then, though plainly achieved, is equally plainly achieved at a cost so high that it cannot be sustained.

Poems like "Fourth of July in Maine," which I will not discuss analytically, and "The Opposite House" seem to me competent, low-keyed meditations—a sort of superior poetic diary-journalism—which exhibit Lowell's poetic motors turning at idling speeds. The title poem, "Near the Ocean," once more hearkens back to *Lord Weary's Castle*, but shows in its penultimate stanza something at least of the older power and force (dissipated in the melodramatic and distinctly stale romanticism of the final stanza, which I will neither quote nor discuss):

> Is it this shore? Their eyes worn white
> as moons from hitting bottom? Night,
> the sandfleas scissoring their feet,
> the sandbed cooling to concrete,
> one borrowed blanket, lights of cars
> shining down at them like stars? . . .
> Sand built the lost Atlantis . . . sand,
> Atlantic ocean, condoms, sand.

But what power there is, here, seems to me clearly tired power and not of the first intensity. This is Lowell rousing himself, struggling against the torpor that has been afflicting his work, and to some extent overcoming it. But only in part.

The poem to which most critics have addressed themselves, in this last of Lowell's middle-period volumes of original poetry, is the first and longest, "Waking Early Sunday Morning." "In [his] earlier poems there was a mounting tension as the self attempted to summon energy to meet the occasion," says R. K. Meiners nicely, but in "Waking Early Sunday Morning," "though we get the reaffirmed wish of the self to break through, if not to tranquility then at least to something like authentic experience, this is accomplished in the somewhat desperate image of the spawning salmon . . . "[20] Meiners goes on to talk of basic assumptions "wearing very thin indeed" and experiential patterns becoming "severely attenuated," with the result that "one of the most interesting movements in his poetry has nearly vanished."[21] And the first stanza of the poem, quoted by Meiners to verify his observations, seems to me to prove his point:

> O to break loose, like the chinook
> salmon jumping and falling back,
> nosing up to the impossible
> stone and bone-crushing waterfall—
> raw-jawed, weak-fleshed there, stopped by ten
> steps of the roaring ladder, and then
> to clear the top on the last try,
> alive enough to spawn and die.

Lowell was, as I have insisted, an excruciatingly honest poet; there is no attempt at concealment, and it is not hard to see what the problems of this poetry are. First of all, though there is a clear ideational link between a man breaking loose and a salmon returning to its natal river in order to spawn, a poetic linkage requires more than mere idea to justify it and, above all, to charge it with feeling and life. It is the poet's job to establish that something more, whether by statement or metaphor or by any other means or combination of means. Lowell simply states the link and then devotes all his flagging energies to describing the salmon—not, let me emphasize, the link, but the salmon pure and simple. But is the salmon as salmon of any particular concern to us, the readers of this poem? If we are conservationists, or fishermen, we will admire the description, perhaps acutely admire it. But even Lowell does not empathize terribly intensely with the salmon. The waterfall up which the salmon must leap, for example, is described as "stone and bone-crushing," which is pretty mechanical. And the salmon itself is described as "raw-jawed, weak-fleshed," which, while it may be accurate, is little more than that. We are told that the ladder has "ten/ steps," which is as far as I know accurate, but why should this detail matter to us? Why indeed is it in the poem? If the line read, instead, "stopped by the/ steps of the roaring ladder," or even "stopped by eight—or seven— or six/ steps of the roaring ladder," in what respect would the poem have changed? And if we are not made to empathize with the spawning salmon, if we are not made to feel some solid link between fish and poet/persona, why should we be affected by the attempted drama of "the last try," or by the statement in the last line quoted, which shows us the salmon up and over, spawning, and then dying?

It is, additionally, a curiously eighteenth-century poem in many features of its diction and verse technique. "The salmon breaks/ water, and now my body wakes . . . " is, for example, almost like something written by the British poet William Cowper (1731–1800)—like Lowell, afflicted with intermittent madness and, like Lowell, given to poems about his own life and surroundings. Or—without going into detailed comparisons—the poem is like something written by yet another pastoralist of the same century, William Shenstone (1714–1763). When Lowell writes lines like "wake of refuse, dacron rope,/ bound for Bermuda or Good Hope," even the rhymes echo back to the eighteenth century. When he writes of "the wine-dark hulls" we are inevitably reminded of still older poets, notably Homer with his famous wine-dark sea. The entire fifth stanza of the poem, it seems to me, would be almost impossible to identify as the work of an American writing in the 1960s:

> I watch a glass of water wet
> with a fine fuzz of icy sweat,
> silvery colors touched with sky,

> serene in their neutrality—
> yet if I shift, or change my mood,
> I see some object made of wood,
> background behind it of brown grain,
> to darken it, but not to stain.

And yet the poem also contains strong echoes of T. S. Eliot ("And now the new electric bells,/ clearly chiming, 'Faith of our fathers,'/ and now the congregation gathers"), pieces of New York patois and Yiddish slang ("explore . . . for . . . dregs and dreck"), and self-conscious invocations of the Muse ("Sing softer!"). Three lines before the final stanza, which is much the best in the poem (and quite properly, from the publisher's point of view, is quoted in full on the book's dust-jacket), things suddenly come to life, with a stark image equal to Lowell's best: "the blind/ swipe of the pruner and his knife/ busy about the tree of life . . . " But though the final stanza is both serious and moving, with its prayer for "peace to our children . . . until the end of time," it is too little, it is too late, and nothing can save the poem or the book, nothing can make either poem or book worthy of our sustained or our continued attention.

4

Prolific Mediocrity and a Final Triumph: Everything Ends with *Day by Day*

I have said that in the last part of his life Lowell published five volumes of original poetry. There are six volumes of original poetry, strictly speaking; I arrive at my slightly reduced total by counting *Notebook* (1970), I think advisedly, as essentially another edition of *Notebook 1967–68* (1969). Lowell's own note to the later book, dated January 1970, speaks of the earlier book as "the first edition" and apologizes for asking "anyone to buy this poem twice. I couldn't stop writing, and have handled my published book as if it were manuscript." In another sense, however, there are only two "books" in this last period. On the one hand, there are all of the assorted *Notebook* poems—which include the poems of *For Lizzie and Harriet*, all of which, "in another order [and] in other versions . . . appeared in . . . *Notebook*," to quote Lowell's note to the volume, and also the poems of *History*, most of which, again according to Lowell, "are taken from my last published poem, *Notebook* [,] begun six years ago"—and the poems of *The Dolphin*, which are I think inseparable from *Notebook* in style and treatment. On the other hand, there are the poems of Lowell's final book, *Day by Day*, published not many days before his death. I will in this chapter use such a division into two "books," the better to analytically approach all the late poetry; it is of course only a question of critical convenience, and in no sense corresponds to the physical facts of publication.

The remarkable fact about the *Notebook*-style poems is how very similar they all are. For one thing, with minor exceptions they are all free-form sonnets, un-rhymed, without the tight inner structures of the true sonnet, and not written in anything like the traditional iambic pentameter metric, but they are fourteen-line poems and obviously sonnet-derived. So consistent, indeed, is this fourteen-line orientation that, beginning the last of these volumes, *The Dolphin*, with an intro-ductory poem in thirteen lines, Lowell concludes with a summary poem in fifteen lines—as if to balance things out. This fourteen-line obsession is distinctly remarkable, not only for Robert Lowell but for any contemporary poet, for we are here dealing with a mass of poetry over 850 printed pages in length, a large mass by any standards. Note, for comparative purposes, that Allen Tate's collected poems come to just over 200 printed pages, Randall Jarrell's and Howard Nemerov's (the latter including verse plays) to 507 printed pages, while such major figures of a slightly earlier generation as e. e. cummings, W. B. Yeats, and T. S. Eliot have their collected poems fitted into books of 458, 454, and 221 pages. Lowell's obsession with this single, relatively short form cannot help but be an extremely significant fact. For comparative purposes, again, I know of no modern obsession with a form that even approaches Lowell's for sheer bulk. The poem of eighteen lines, in three irregularly-rhymed stanzas, worked out by John Berryman for his "dream songs," is perhaps the closest analogue, comprising 385 poems in the two primary volumes, plus a few additional examples written later on.[1] And we are still speaking, even for close to 400 formally similar Berryman poems, of a mass of printed pages not much larger than 400, or roughly half the bulk of Lowell's one-form poems.

And the similarity of Lowell's free-form sonnets, one to the other, is not simply a matter of formal considerations. There is what I can only call an astonishing uniformity about this huge spilling-out of short poems, a similarity of tone, of diction, of vocabulary, a choppiness of rhythm, an overall flatness of affect. "I have sat and listened to too many/ words of the collaborating muse," says Lowell truthfully, in the last poem of the last *Notebook*-style book, *The Dolphin*. And in another poem in the same book he declares, "I would change my trueself if I could:/ I am doubtful . . . uncertain my big steps./ . . . tried spirits sigh,/ doing nothing the day because they think/ imagination matures from doing nothing,/ hoping for choice, the child of vacillation." Indeed, in the "Afterthought" to *Notebook* he makes it perfectly explicit: in some degree he knew he had lost his way and, for all the vast outpouring, could not readily find it again:

A poet can be intelligent and on to what he does; yet he walks, half-balmy and over-armored—caught by his amnesia, ignorance and education. For the poet without direction, poetry is a way of not saying what he has to say.

And in *The Dolphin*, once again, he reproduces snatches from the letters of his second wife, Elizabeth Hardwick, to much the same purpose. Lowell, she says, is "someone fighting unreality—/ love vanquished by his mysterious carelessness." Here is yet another comment by Elizabeth Hardwick: "*You can't carry your talent with you like a suitcase./ . . . do you really* know *what you have done?*" In life, perhaps not: "I've closed my mind/ so long, I want to keep it closed, perhaps," Lowell writes, once more in *The Dolphin*. But I am inclined to think that he had some idea, as a poet, of what he had done, that he was to some extent on to what he was doing, that at least in part he knew himself, in these poems, to be a "poet without direction."

But Lowell's self-knowledge, or lack of it, is of course not the issue and is in the final analysis not terribly important. The fact remains that, despite a good deal of critical acclaim (some of it, naturally, little more than puffery, but a good deal of it sincere), virtually all the *Notebook*-style poems are rather dull, rarely falling below the standard level, rarely rising above it. It may be that Lowell's incessant revising, and reordering, and then revising and reordering again, reflects his own awareness of that fundamental poetic flatness, that monotonous lack of poetic interest. That too is not the issue, though it may well bear on it. "I have taken from many books," says the prose note to *Notebook 1967–68*, "used the throwaway conversational inspirations of my friends, and much more that I idly spoke to myself." Exactly: the almost nine hundred pages amount to a kind of gigantic grab bag, yet another desperate, flaying attack on the windmills of reality. The brief prefatory note to *History* confirms what everything else has already made clear: "My old title [for these poems], *Notebook*, was more accurate than I wished, i.e. the composition was jumbled." And he adds, wistfully and not I think very hopefully, "I hope this jumble or jungle is cleared—that I have cut the waste marble from the figure." But honesty is unfortunately not enough, and reality does not succumb to desperate assaults, no matter how prolonged, no matter how intense.

Here is one of the sonnets from *Notebook 1967–68*, "Elisabeth Schwarzkopf in New York," reprinted unchanged in *Notebook*, and reprinted with some changes in *History*. I will deal with the original poem first, and then with the changes.

> Yet people live here . . . Paris, Wien, Milano,
> which had more genius, grace, preoccupations?
> We pass up grace, our entrance fee and tithe
> for dwelling in the heavenly Jerusalem—
> small price for salience, and the world is here:

Elisabeth Schwarzkopf sings, herself her parts,
Wo ist Silvia and *die Marschallin*,
until the rivers of the early world,
the Hudson and the Tigris, burst their bar,
trembling like water-ivy down the spine,
from the satyr's tussock to his hardened hoof—
la Diva, crisped, remodeled for the boards,
roughs it with chaff and cardigan at recordings,
is anyone's single and useful weekend guest.

This is not bad poetry; neither is it good poetry. The
technical mixture is an odd one, as it is throughout these
poems. We have the casual, slightly snotty journalism
of the New York culture-vulture—it is New York which
is here called, tongue-in-cheek, "the heavenly Jerusalem"—the name-dropping, the easy familiarity with
internationally acclaimed singers like Elisabeth Schwarzkopf, and with her repertoire, songs like
"Where is Sylvia?" and the Richard Strauss role she so
often sang in the opera *Der Rosenkavalier*. This is
replaced, beginning in line 8, with four much more
"poetic" lines, pretentiously trying to link New York's
Hudson River with one of the great waterways of early
civilization in the Middle East and full of meaningless
references to satyrs and the like. In what way, exactly,
is the Hudson like the Tigris? How is the Hudson to be
understood as a river "of the early world"? Nothing is
said about such things, and it does not matter, for plainly
the poet is not deeply engaged with his own mythologizing chatter. How does the satyr fit into this poem?
Why are we told, so very specifically, of "water-ivy"?
Again, it does not matter, and there is no reason to take
it seriously. Having lapsed into the symbol-chucking of
his earliest poetry, though in a much more subdued
fashion, Lowell just as casually drifts back to the high-
society, insider gossip, reporting—quite accurately, as
it happens—on the career revivification of the famous
soprano. I do not know if the last statement, concerning

Miss Schwarzkopf's role as a weekend guest is or is not
accurate, nor do I care: these are subjects for gossip
magazines, not for poets and critics of poets. Absent
some poetic reason for the reader to be involved in such
matters, some true working of the material, why indeed
ought the reader to feel any more involvement than he
might with, say, a well-written piece in the *New York
Times* (which Lowell was obviously himself reading)?

I chose this poem for discussion, as it happens,
simply by flexing the book and opening it entirely at
random. There would be very little difference had I
chosen another poem. The changes, in a sense improving
the poem, nonetheless do not I believe improve it very
much. Here is the new opening (the only other changes
are "like" for "is," in the final line, which is strictly a
matter of syntactical smoothing, and a river-switch I will
comment on in a moment):

> The great still fever for Paris, Vienna, Milan;
> which had more genius, grace, preoccupations?
> Loss of grace is bagatelle to pay
> for a niche in the Pantheon or New York—
> and as for Europe, they could bring it with them.

This is on the whole tighter, as well as distinctly
smoother. The snotty "Wien, Milano" is quietly replaced
by standard English usages, "Vienna, Milan"; the fifth
line is more accessible; "bagatelle" is hardly a thrilling
coinage, but it is both clearer and freer of unnecessary
connotations than "our entrance fee and tithe." But does
the Pantheon have any more place in this poem than
does "the heavenly Jerusalem"? There is surely more
point to substituting the Danube for the Tigris, deflating
the mythological to the sensible and logical; "the rivers
of the early world" now properly become "the historic
rivers of both worlds." On the other hand, while the
original opening words of the poem, "Yet people live
here," are admittedly not exploited properly, they do

have a degree of pungency that seems to me lacking in
the rather strained "The great still fever." And, overall,
I do not believe there is much more poetic energy, or
emotion, or meaning in the revised poem than there
was in the first version.

Comparing Lowell's love sequence, *For Lizzie and
Harriet* (Lizzie is Elizabeth Hardwick; Harriet, their
daughter), to one of the Victorian era's similar sequences,
George Meredith's *Modern Love*, Steven Gould Axelrod
is forced to conclude that while *"For Lizzie and Harriet*
is often quite touching in its depiction of human frailty
and desire, . . . yet it possesses nothing like the emotional power and essential seriousness of Meredith's
great sequence."[2] The tenor of the comment seems to
me every bit as revealing as what is being said, for I too
find myself wanting to think better of these poems, and
of Lowell generally, than in fact I am able to do. Helen
Vendler's sensitive reaction to the *Notebook*-style poetry,
which I want to quote at some length, is even more
revealing:

His sonnets throw up nearly indigestible fragments of experience, unprefaced by explanation, unexplained by cause or
result; sudden soliloquies of figures from Biblical times to
contemporary history; translations; diary jottings; stately imitations of known forms; the whole litter and debris and detritus
of a mind absorptive for fifty years. His free association,
irritating at first, hovering always dangerously toward the point
where unpleasure replaces pleasure, nonetheless becomes
bearable, and then even deeply satisfying, on repeated reading.
. . . The presence of the familiar, and the genuineness of its
note, act to assure the genuineness of the rest.[3]

I think it is fair to say that we can virtually see, as we
read this, Professor Vendler struggling to make herself
like these poems, struggling to overcome "unpleasure,"
struggling not to be "irritated" by assorted failures and
incompetencies. It is an honorable struggle, as Lowell
is an honorable poet, and Professor Vendler ultimately

bows to her desire to like the unlikeable, to respect the
respectable but uninspired. I have tried to do the same,
for pretty much identical reasons, but cannot. It seems
to me that Axelrod, on the whole a much less brilliant
critic than Professor Vendler, is quite simply right when
he says, speaking of *History* but for my purposes speaking
of all the *Notebook*-style poems, that "Lowell holds
something of himself back. *History*, replete with intellectual power, lacks emotional power."[4] Axelrod yields
to much the same temptation that Vendler succumbs to,
calling *The Dolphin*—as distinct from the other *Notebook*-style poems—a "magnificent poem of consciouness
. . . ."[5] *The Dolphin* can surely be distinguished from
the other *Notebook*-style books, but only because its
subjects and its themes can be distinguished; the poetry
is unfortunately the same. Here, for example, is the
conclusion of a poem on the great Jewish psychiatrist,
Sigmund Freud:

> What do we care for the great man of culture—
> Freud's relations were liquidated at Belsen,
> Moses Cohn who had nothing to offer culture
> was liquidated at Belsen. Must we die,
> living in places we have learned to live in,
> completing the only work we're trained to do?

Freud was released by the Nazis and permitted to go to
London; his international standing protected and pre-
served him. There is deep irony, and enormous food for
reflection, in the German sparing of Sigmund Freud and
murdering of Moses Cohn, and six million other European Jews "who had nothing to offer culture." As a Jew
myself, I would be the last to deny the need for endless
reflection, confronted with such matters—not to mention
a resort to irony. But where is the poetic power, where
is the poetic energy? How are we as readers of this poem
involved, moved? "Readers who demand something
more than the eye's verbatim transcript," argues Pro-

fessor Vendler, "who do not ask whether in fact there
is anything more, may not find these poems heartbreak-
ing."[6] Lowell's own heart may have been broken; plainly,
as she testifies, he wanted his readers' hearts to be
broken. But is there "in fact . . . anything more" in the
poetry than "the eye's verbatim transcript"? Vendler
exclaims, fiercely loyal to the man she calls "our greatest
contemporary poet," "It is astonishing that anyone confronted with Lowell's three volumes of sonnets [*History*,
For Lizzie and Harriet, and *The Dolphin*] should still be
praising *Lord Weary's Castle* over *History*."[7] She be-
lieves that "the instinctive principles on which he worked
will become clearer with time."[8] Hers is an immensely
generous defense, but it does not, it cannot persuade,
not in the face of the contradictory evidence of the
poetry itself. Readers of the future are not likely to
ignore Robert Lowell, but neither are they likely to
focus for long on any of the *Notebook*-style poems, in
any of their versions, from any of their volumes.

Lowell's final book of original poetry, *Day by Day*,
published in 1977 just before the poet's sudden death,
is exceedingly different from the *Notebook*-style poetry.
Most obviously, it no longer hammers away in the almost
monomaniacal single-form approach of the other late
volumes—and the attempt to ram through is, as I have
said of Lowell's earlier work, not an approach that seems
ever to have worked for him.[9] The very fact that he
struggled so long, so hard, and so insistently to force his
way down the free-form sonnet road is significant, and
in terms of the immediate results of the struggle it is
clearly unfortunate. But in the very last years of his life
he abruptly gave up that futile attempt, and turned out
the frequently glowingly beautiful poems of *Day by Day*.
His *Notebook*-style poetry was going nowhere; on the
other hand, for all the futility, for all their waste of time
and energy, perhaps these ineffectual poems were ac-

tually necessary. Perhaps he had to make the attempt
to create a large narrative out of pieces all the same size,
had to force himself to work the long-poem and the
political-poem ambition out of his system. He had done
almost that once before, with *The Mills of the Kavanaughs;* the result, in a sense, of that massive failure had
been *Life Studies. Notebook 1967–68* and its revision,
Notebook, are supplied with a page of "Dates," a table
of the external, public events around which he tried to
group and order his poems. The referents of the poems
in *Day by Day,* just as those in *Life Studies,* are almost
exclusively internal. These are largely personal poems,
and the experience they are founded in is largely his
own. Whether Lowell would or could have gone on from
this last book, as he could not go on from *Life Studies,*
no one can say: *Day by Day's* glow, in some measure,
is the result of Lowell's abiding sense of his imminent
death. In that sense, indeed, the aura of an unfinished
life's work inevitably hangs over the book, and over the
reader of it. But I do not think it matters a great deal
whether *Day by Day,* when the critical dust has finally
settled, is ranked below, above, or on the same plane
as *Life Studies.* It is still too new to me, as is Lowell's
death, for me to feel secure and final in my own
evaluation of it. I rank it very high; whether it is a
capstone to a life's work or, as I tend to think, a
movement into something new, and different, and un-
knowably better, it is a book to be read and savored
with great and loving care.

The best way to examine *Day by Day,* I believe, is
not to dwell on its failures, not to examine it for poems
that resemble *Lord Weary's Castle*—and there are
some—or *Life Studies*—there are rather a lot—or indeed
to deal with the great majority of poems that are clear
and good but in no important way different from, or
advances on, the best poems of *Life Studies.* There is a
handful of poems that represent, I think, serious forward

progress, as also there are other poems which, in this detail or that, confirm that forward movement. And it is·exclusively that handful I want now to consider in some detail. There are, in my view, a total of nine such "new" poems, new in the sense that they seem to take new approaches to the creation of poetry (though other contemporary American poets have used aspects of this new approach, before Lowell), and they are all in part three of the book, subtitled "Day by Day" and dedicated, retrospectively, "for Caroline." They are, in the order they occur in the book, "Suburban Surf," "Turtle," "Seventh Year," "Shaving," "Three Freuds," "Home," "Notice," "Shifting Colors," and the final poem, "Epilogue." (The brief appendix contains three translations, none of which seem to me to add to the argument of either this chapter or the next, which will deal with *Imitations*.)

"Suburban Surf," subtitled "After Caroline's return," the first of the new-style poems, appears on page 96 of a volume that, appendix of translations aside, contains 127 pages. Its swift, blunt, uncluttered power is immediately apparent: "You lie in my insomniac arms,/ as if you drank sleep like coffee."[10] This is the first strophe, complete and entire, and that sparseness alone is something new and different in Lowell's verse. But more importantly, there is a powerful sense of everything that is needful having been said—and not a syllable more. Lowell's early prolixity, in point of fact, never left him; even in *Day by Day*, and certainly in every other book he published, there are wordy passages, eminently cuttable. In his use of adjectives, in particular, he often committed the jarring mistake of adding colors and intensifiers and explanations when nothing more was needed, when, indeed, the intrusion of unnecessary material and unnecessary emphasis succeeded only in subtracting from rather than adding to the effect. "Suburban Surf" opens so pointedly, and with so unerring a sense of its own focus, its own true center and core, that the reader at once senses poetic power and poetic procedure tightly controlled, firmly marshaled and mutually cooperative. But a Robert Lowell *not* fighting against himself—as stubbornly, even perversely, he has so often done—would indeed be a new Robert Lowell, and the reader who knows his earlier work cannot help also wondering, it seems to me, if such control, such harmoniousness of message and instrumentality, can be maintained.

Let me set out the next seven lines, which I think provide a stunningly positive answer to that nagging question:

Then,
like a bear tipping a hive for honey,
you shake the pillow for French cigarettes.

No conversation—
then suddenly as always cars
helter-skelter for feed like cows—

suburban surf come alive . . .

Lineation, here—the one-word line, "Then"—couples with the other vectors of the poem and not only maintains but in fact accelerates—and properly accelerates—the swift movement of the verse. The simile of the following line, gentle and loving but wonderfully off-key at the same time, as befitting the reunion of a married couple whose marriage has gone very sour very recently, is one Lowell might well have imagined earlier on. But earlier on he would never have left well enough alone; he would have embroidered and dithered; he would have half-worried the image into the ground. He leaves it at once, here, but also carries it into the next line, the next frame of the poem, where it informs and adds both warmth and an odd humor to the woman's post-coital hunt for cigarettes—and the adjective, "French," is a perfect touch, in no way intrusive. It says a great deal, and says it neither heavily nor even nastily, though it is in the end a negatively-tinged comment. This frame too is swiftly completed; we are swung into yet another short strophe, and greeted with an almost machine-gun abruptness: "No conversation." How the earlier Lowell would have filled in and fussed over that notion! He leaves it at once; it has done its work. Vehicular traffic has often been a jarring reminder of modern urban civilization, in his poems; it serves in that role here, but, having established the idea, he yet once more sprints past it, opening out and amplifying with different, expansive, rather than merely additive material: the cars' motion becomes "suburban surf come alive."

There is some uncertainty, some slight verbal insistence, in the lines that follow. But that seems to me less important than the fact that, in the final eight lines, Lowell reasserts the tight, swift mastery of the poem's opening:

A false calm is the best calm.

In noonday light,
the cars are tin, stereotype and bright,
a farce
of their former selves at night—
invisible as exhaust,
personal as animals.

Gone
the sweet agitation of the breath of Pan.

From the magisterial-sounding paradox of "A false calm is the best calm," nicely set off by itself, a strophe of just the one line, Lowell springs back to the earlier image of the suburban cars nosing up and down. But he does not overdo the image, as he does not lean with his old ferocity on the adjectives. The "light," for example, is "noonday," no more. The cars themselves are "tin," are "stereotype," are "bright," all adjectives that calmly and yet accurately say what needs to be said. Having said it,

tinkling a brassy rhyme-bell the while ("light/bright"),
he moves rapidly on, telling us of the day/night contrast
in newly taut, sparse language (and giving the rhyme-
bell yet another shake), then quickly, strongly ties the
image up with a powerful brief summary, "invisible as
exhaust . . . " The metaphor is quiet, but it evokes
exactly the right combination of physical intangibility
and poisonousness. "Personal as animals" is perhaps a
shade too bald, but it is not given a chance to undercut
the poem's momentum. Lowell immediately breaks to
the short final strophe, asserts the poem's stark flavor
with a one-word line, "Gone," and then glides lightly
into the gentle sadness of the ending, "the sweet agitation
of the breath of Pan." The pagan reference, to a goat
god of notably priapic inclinations, is both muted and
neatly effective, not claiming too much, not trying to
unsay what must, in spite of all that is positive in their
coupling, still be said. "The sweet breath of Pan" can
persuade, for the moment, but in the end their love like
their marriage is "Gone."

"Turtle," a slightly longer poem, is a genuine
phantasmagoria, a nightmare poem stated in simple and
therefore remarkably chilling language. A childhood
hunter of turtles, Lowell first sees himself as "an old
turtle,/ absentminded, inelastic,/ kept afloat by losing
touch," then steps back a bit and gives us half a dozen
lines about turtles as turtles, concluding: "Snapping
turtles only submerge./ They have survived . . . not by
man's philanthrophy." A quick-paced strophe of twelve
lines takes us another step back, this time into childhood,
and shows us the unthinking young turtle-hunter, who
"could have lost a finger" but didn't, who instead grew
up to become, in the next strophe, the adult sleeper
newly awake and unable to tell real from dream. He
sees "three snapping turtles squatted on my drifting
clothes," one "a puppy squeaking and tweaking/ my
empty shirt for milk." The moving, determinedly un-

sentimental picture gives way, immediately, to one more
threatening, in the next strophe's first lines: "They are
stale and panting;/ what is dead in me wakes their
appetite." Turtles and savage schoolmates flicker, blend:
"crooked miles/ and high-school nicknames on their
tongues." "Nothing has passed between us but time,"
the strophe concludes, a passionate but starkly stated
affirmation of human nothingness, human transience.
And now, for the first and only time, the turtles speak;
there is no overt menace in their words, but what they
say is chilling:

> "You've wondered where we were these years?
> Here are we."

I could have wished the second of these lines to be less
literary and more colloquial, but again the faint damp-
ening is not permitted to take hold. Lowell breaks into
the final and terrifying strophe:

> They lie like luggage—
> my old friend the turtle . . . Too many pictures
> have screamed from the reel . . . in the rerun,
> the snapper holds on till sunset—
> in the awful instantness of retrospect,
> its beak
> works me underwater drowning by my neck,
> as it claws away pieces of my flesh
> to make me small enough to swallow.

What Lowell has begun to learn, it seems to me, is that
words are enough, have power to say what they are
given to say. There is no need to pile layers and then
still more layers of overwrought action and thought on
top of the bare, sufficient reality. Indeed, it is precisely
that reality that truly carries the power, both of ideas
and of emotions. To wrap it in abstractions and poke it
with sticks in order to make it writhe more vividly is to
kill it, not to quicken it. And he has learned, just as
importantly, to weave his poetic fabric out of one cloth,

not many—and to keep the movement of his verse free
and swift, clean and always aimed at its target.

"Seventh Year," the poem immediately following,
again has the structural movement, though not the overt
trappings, of a phantasmagoria. Looking back at his failed
third marriage, and the other failures associated with it,
Lowell leaps from perspective to perspective, first the
ancient family seat he and Caroline occupied in England,
then "Longfellow's house on Brattle Street," in Boston,
then to the American poet Hart Crane, dead by his own
hand, and finally to himself "swaying at the end of [a]
party/ a half-filled glass in each hand." There are logical
connections, first house to house, and then poet to poet
to poet (himself); there are also sensate, deeply-felt
connections, perhaps best expressed in the one-line
penultimate strophe, "To each the rotting natural to his
age," as fine a line as I think anyone has ever written.
Milgate, the British house, unnamed here but cited by
name elsewhere in this and in earlier volumes, is
described lovingly on the whole, though threatened,
somewhat absurdly, by "burnished oxweight cows,"
which "crash/ foot over foot through vine and glass."
Lowell sees the house and the "instantly dispelled/
dream of putting [it] on its feet" as definitively, terminally
disposed of: "instantly dispelled" comes in the first line,
and conditions everything that follows. "I see it clearly,"
he informs us with sober, succinct realism, "but with
the blind glass eyes of a doll." The insufficiently cared
for, insufficiently caring cows, damaging grounds and
house impartially, are last shown to us, "lowing to one
another with the anxious/ human voice of a boy calling
cows." The reversal of expectation, and of natural order,
is swift and effective, leading neatly and easily to another
old house, once, a very long time ago, inhabited by
another aging poet, like Lowell himself a New Englander.
In "Longfellow's house," today, now, we are informed

pungently, "only his bearded bust of Zeus,/ his schoolday self, is young." Rot is then made suddenly more potent, and more grisly: "the long face" of the older poet's first wife, burned to death in a horrible accidental fire, "ages as if alive/ as Longfellow . . . " Both are now dead, of course, but even in life Longfellow had in some parts of himself died when she died; they are both statues in this poem, as well as inhabitants of the old house. The pathos and the muted desperation come together in the next strophe: "The New England Augustans/ lived so long one thought/ the snow of their hair would never melt."

The shift, on the face of it abrupt, to "Where is Hart Crane,/ the disinherited, the fly by night," is of course not at all abrupt. The whole thrust of the Longfellow passages, concluding with the invocation of the now-vanished "New England Augustans," has been to establish, implicitly, the notion of *ubi sunt*, "where are . . . ?" The question is of course traditionally not a question, but a rhetorical way of making a backward-glancing statement. Hart Crane was disinherited both by his family and, in a deeper sense, by American culture, and he was, as a tormented, alcoholic homosexual, distinctly a "fly by night." Dionysus is of course a god of both alcohol and of ecstasy, and his link with the Greek poetic drama gives him strong literary associations. Just as "fly by night" contains a very probable pun on Crane's then-illicit sexuality, so too does the assertion that Crane "gave/ the drunken Dionysus firmer feet." Crane was, in a word, an ecstatic poet, and a good one, Lowell here tells us. "To each the rotting natural to his age," he says laconically—and I think so devastatingly that I cannot refrain from again quoting the line. And then back to Lowell himself, yet another poet, back again in the old house he dreamed of restoring—but "never again"—and drunk, though not exactly Dionysuslike, at the end of a party, "dividing the minute we

cannot prolong"—none of us, poet or partygoer. The
leaping identification in the final three lines is probably
deliberately indeterminate. Is "they" in the final line
the other people at the party? Or is it the other poets?
And does it matter, since for Lowell it is the identity
and not the dissimilarity that strikes out at him: "I too
swayed/ by the hard infatuate wind of love/ they cannot
hear." It is more than likely the dead poets to whom he
refers, though as I say I am not sure. The "swaying"
produced by drink is neatly joined to a more eternal but
less physical swaying, stronger than that induced by
alcohol. The restrained, precise use of adjectives is
particularly impressive. As I said earlier in this chapter,
Lowell through most of his career over-used, and sometimes inappropriately used, adjectives, trying to over-
intensify what he did not consider intense enough as it
stood. Here, he tells us that the "wind of love," surely
as delicate and yet as insistent a metaphor as he has ever
employed, is first of all "hard," which is to say both
strong and harsh, and then that it is "infatuate," which
is to say foolish and extravagant. There is not a particle
of exaggeration in either of these adjectival descriptions.
Together they shape a sense of irresistible and yet
unguidable, unguided power that expresses precisely
what is wanted.

I can be somewhat briefer, by this point, with most
of the remaining new poems. "Shaving," which follows
"Seventh Year" and concludes this first grouping (of my
devising, to be sure, rather than Lowell's), begins as if
it will be a solitary self-portrait, founded on the plain
truth that "shaving's the one time I see my face . . . "
But after concluding that, "For me, a stone is as
inflammable as a paper match," Lowell widens the
perspective to include Caroline, and to deftly contrast
their divergent natures:

> The household comes to a stop—
> you too, head bent,

> inking, crossing out . . . frowning
> at times with a face open as a sunflower.

> We are lucky to have done things as one.

Again, in these new poems Lowell does not stop to dot
his i's and cross his t's. Caroline too is a writer, engaged
in writing and revising. So much is similar, and "the
household" inevitably "comes to a stop" when they are
both at work (or when she is at work and he is ill). But
hers is a "face open as a sunflower." That is all he needs
to say, and all he says. Given such temperamental
extremes, the last line, a strophe of its own, follows with
simple, clear force. No poetic embroidery is needed or
attempted; the verse movement is not so much accel-
erated as, in all these new poems, natural and swift.

"Three Freuds," somewhat later in the volume (two
fine intervening poems, "Ten Minutes" and "Visitors,"
seem to me too imbued with older approaches for this
discussion to include them) is a remarkable little poem,
twenty-four short lines so neatly constructed that, at the
end, we are almost surprised at how effortlessly Lowell
has laid in, and then rounded off, his dramatic confrontation. We begin with the poet-persona, clearly Lowell,
entering a faintly mocked-at structure known as *"The
Priory,"* in front of which stands a statue of "dear, dead
old Dr. Wood blanche-white," the founder of what, a
few lines farther along, turns out to be a mental asylum.
"He looks like Freud . . . " and "Inside the window, is
a live patient,/ a second bearded Freud,/ no Freud
. . . ," and this one, "not artificial," stands on line "at
the cold buffet/ to pluck up coleslaw in his hands." We
have our three Freuds, the real one and these two
resemblances; we also have the backdrop fully laid in,
the aura of self-indulgence, of almost willful dottiness;
and in the last four lines, italicized to indicate that this
is another speaker, someone addressing the poem's first
speaker, we have the dramatic confrontation: *"When you
emerge/ it may seem too late./ You choose to go/ where*

you knew I could not follow." The speaker seems to be
Caroline; the message is devastatingly plain.

"Home," which follows, is much longer and takes
place inside the asylum. (The poems of *Life Studies*, no
less autobiographical, did not have the flexibility, the
necessary capacity to omit as well as to include; they
could not trace out, as these new poems can, the fullness
of the experience.) "Our ears put us in touch with things
unheard of," it begins, casting a quick, wide net, and
then just as quickly drawing it in again: "the trouble is
the patients are tediously themselves . . . " The same
counterpointing, light-footed and merciless, is used
throughout the poem. Someone, probably a doctor,
observes " 'Remarkable breakdown, remarkable recov-
ery'," and then, after a swift dash, the poet continues:
"but the breakage can go on repeating/ once too often."
And this in turn is followed by an italicized, two-line
strophe spoken (or thought) unidentifiably: *"Why is it so
hard for them to accept/ the very state of happiness is
wrong?"* After more about the hospital and about his
coming to it, the poem ends with a long, confessedly
mad "dialogue/ between the devil and myself,/ not knowing which is which or worse . . . " Picking up on a
reference to saying a Hail Mary, the last five lines focus,
without other preparation needed, on what seems to be
another of the mad patients:

> The Queen of Heaven, I miss her,
> we were divorced. She never doubted
> the divided, stricken soul
> could call her Maria,
> and rob the devil with a word.

But "The Queen of Heaven" is also, surely, a reference
to one of his ex-wives, probably Jean Stafford, of his
three wives the most Catholic by far. The ambiguity is
part and parcel of the madness that lies at the center of
the poem. And yet the marital linkage also deepens,

strengthens, and makes much more moving the portrait of the hopeless and for all that the despairing poet-persona. Again, none of Lowell's poetry before *Day by Day* could so effectively combine these disparate elements, these conflicting and yet linked cross-references; the asylum poems in the *Notebook*-style seem as flat as pancakes by comparison, but even the great mass of poems in *Life Studies* also seem flatter, less potent, than these darting, surefooted new creations.

"Notice," another short poem, starts once more in the asylum and quickly draws out the helplessness of proferred medical help. " 'These days of only poems and depressions', " the poet asks of the doctor, "what can I do with them? Will they help me to notice/ what I cannot bear to look at?' " Neither doctor nor poet answers; the poem leaps through time, and through space on the page, to a new strophe, with the poet, now "cured," crowded onto a "rush-hour train." He scribbles, poeticizing, "on the back of a letter," lines descriptive of trees emerging from winter barrenness, explaining that, now cured, he is free to thus scribble, free to know "that the much-heralded spring is here," free to ask, of no one in particular, " 'Is this what you would call a blossom?' " It is a stark and yet poignant portrayal: though the madhouse scene is supposed to be behind him, "the doctor . . . forgotten now/ like a friend's wife's maiden-name," the juxtaposition of stanzas descriptive of life within and without the asylum is subtly underlined by the drifting, unfocussed, helplessly observing mind of the poet-persona in either place—which is to say, in any place. The poem ends: "Then home—I can walk it blindfold./ But we must notice—/ we are designed for the moment." Uncertainty of focus here joins with uncertainty of tenure; the poet is as I have said sharply aware, throughout this book, of his own human impermanence. There is a jaunty unreality, quite deliberate, I think, to "I can walk it blindfold," an unreality

emphasized at once by the swift swing away from such
proud fatuousness to the final caveat—as if to say, yes,
of course you can walk it blindfold, but what does that
count for, eh?

The following poem, "Shifting Colors," presents us
with the poet-persona fishing and ruminating, as he looks
around him, from object to object, and especially from
observed animal to observed animal. Weary of fishing,
which is perhaps a medically prescribed form of restful
activity ("self-torture," he calls it), he finds himself
"ready to paint/ lilacs or confuse a thousand leaves,/ as
landscapists must." And it is as a kind of poetic landscapist
that he evolves the poem. "All day my miscast troutfly
buzzes about my ears/ and empty mind," he notes near
the end, having earlier interjected the comment, carefully linked to his quick series of animal visions and
comparisons, "Poor measured, neurotic man—/ animals
are more instinctive virtuosi." The animals are sexual;
he is not, "too weak to strain to remember, or give/
recollection the eye of a microscope." What he sees, the
penultimate strophe assures us, is only "description
without significance,/ transcribed verbatim by my eye."
But though he goes on to claim that "This is not the
directness that catches/ everything on the run and then
expires," it is in truth exactly that. After long striving,
Lowell has captured the kind of quick pen possessed by
Pablo Picasso—or something that begins to approximate
it. He is not fully sure of himself, nor is he as successful
as was Picasso, whose every line radiates meaning and
form and design. "I would write only in response to the
gods," he declares majestically; the wish would seem to
have been very close to realization. And then he concludes the poem, conscious as every working artist is of
the burden as well as the glory of his art, " . . . like
Mallarmé who had the good fortune/ to find a style that
made writing impossible." This is to be sure serious, but
not literally serious. Consider only the extraordinary

devotion Lowell had to his work, the plain fact of year after year of slogging away at it. "Lowell lived for writing," Professor Vendler records, "was never happier than, as he said, when revising his revisions."[11] This is the farthest thing from whining, though there are distinct flashes of self-pity in *Day by Day*: it is not easy to know that you are drawing closer and closer to death, not just by the facts of time alone, but also by the processes of heart disease. I do not think I am being overgenerous when I call these last lines of "Shifting Colors" noble, as well as new.

Three poems more—one, "Unwanted," is so exceedingly close to the bone, so directly drawn from life, without a good deal of poetic mediation, that it scarcely seems like poetry—brings us to the final new poem, and the final poem in the volume, appropriately titled "Epilogue." It is retrospective, but not in an autobiographical sense. Rather, it is a sort of interim *ars poetica*, an attempt to sum up, largely for himself I suspect, where he had gotten to with his art, and where he might be able to go. It is also extremely fine poetry:

> Those blessèd structures, plot and rhyme—
> why are they no help to me now
> I want to make
> something imagined, not recalled?

There is a new sort of elegance in these apparently simply stated lines. The deliberate archaism of "blessèd" fits, like everything here, seamlessly well with what is being said: unobtrusive form and straightforward diction, propelled by light, swift verse rhythms, carry the reader urgently forward, and at the same time involve him. Lowell's honesty is both more fully apparent, now, and more attractive; it is not being pushed at us, but only offered. The poem continues:

> I hear the noise of my own voice:
> *The painter's vision is not a lens,*

> *it trembles to caress the light.*
> But sometimes everything I write
> with the threadbare art of my eye
> seems a snapshot,
> lurid, rapid, garish, grouped,
> heightened from life,
> yet paralyzed by fact.
> All's misalliance.
> Yet why not say what happened?

He recognizes, as of course he must, that art is not photography; he also recognizes the perils of the twentieth-century artist, working out of his own limited, merely personal experience. Triviality, mere "snapshot," can all too easily be the result. The artist can "heighten," intensify that experience, but if he stays too close to it, if he is not enough of an artist to achieve distance and some larger view, his work will be "paralyzed by fact." Suspecting, accordingly, that "all's misalliance," Lowell simultaneously finds himself obliged to push on: "Yet why not say what happened?"

> Pray for the grace of accuracy
> Vermeer gave to the sun's illumination
> stealing like the tide across a map
> to his girl solid with yearning.

I think "stealing like the tide" is too easy, rather slack; the rest of the passage strikes the fully elegant tones of what has gone before, and what will follow. "The grace of accuracy" is doubly notable for its clear forcefulness and also, I believe, for what it says, implicitly, about Lowell's earlier, frenzied religiosity. He was never meant to be anything but a secular, albeit a spiritually oriented, writer.

> We are poor passing facts,
> warned by that to give

> each figure in the photograph
> his living name.

It is perhaps hard for anyone not a practicing poet to realize what "grace of accuracy," what tremendous power of precise concision, Lowell achieves in such lines. The "color" words, here, are deeply restrained—incredibly restrained, in comparison to his earlier practice. "Poor passing facts" is at one and the same time a clear, simple assertion and also, by its flavor, its tone, its rhetoric, an allusion to, and a bow to, older poets in a straight line back to William Shakespeare; the phrase is plainly more than a little Shakespearean, without being in any sense archaic. "Warned," the next "color" word, is admonitory, but gently: Lowell is no longer pushing. And the nature of the warning, plainly asserted, is the obligation to see straight and call "each figure in the photograph/ [by] his living name." The third color word, obviously, is "living," and therein lies the deepest key to this new poetry, as it must be also the key to any and all poetry of the highest order. But to get at the "living name" is no easy task, no matter how easy it may be to formulate the task. Some artists struggle all their lives, and vainly, to strip away the layers that interfere between artist and that living essence, that living reality, that simple, basic truth. Some artists proclaim themselves as standing at that still center; they are usually lying, though they are not always found out. Lowell has never been a liar, but neither did he ever find it easy to get through the layers and layers in which his living names, his reality, was wrapped. I do not mean to be dramatic, but it seems to me both the glory and the pity of *Day by Day* that Lowell was working his way through the final layers, was even perhaps intermittently through to that living center, when he gave us this final book. His death has, for the moment at least, apparently stifled genuine critical attention for *Day by Day*. A sensitive critic, preferably someone who is himself a poet, could I believe easily devote an entire volume to an analysis of what the book offers us, what the book shows us, what the book tells us. This book, and this poet-critic, cannot do more, now, than they have done.

5

Picking Pebbles Out
of Foreign Sand: *Imitations*

Imitations, published in 1961, has had remarkably little understanding and, on the whole, a poor press. Since it looks very like a volume of translations, the great majority of critical response has been, mistakenly, that it is in fact a volume of translations. Lowell himself, to be sure, is at least in part responsible for the confusion. Despite the disclaimer implicit in the title, despite the long list of freedoms and licences recorded in his prefatory remarks, and despite even the frank and truthful admission that "This book was written from time to time when I was unable to do anything of my own," there is also a good deal about the book's arrangement, and even about Lowell's prefatory remarks, that make *Imitations* seem to be what it is not, namely a book of what are usually called translations. And this more or less deliberate ambivalence records, honestly, a confusion of purpose which I believe Lowell did suffer from. He was I think never sure, in working with material from other languages, quite what he was doing. Was he translating, as so many people thought, and many still think? Was he adapting, or "imitating," as he usually tried to call what he was up to? (The phrase comes from that great seventeenth-century translator and critic, John Dryden [1621–1700], who was of course also one of the leading poets of his period.) And this confusion, finally, makes more than sense, in the larger context of Lowell's career as a whole. It fits like a glove, as I shall now attempt to make clear.

As I have indicated, Lowell's academic training was substantial, and largely literary. He majored in classics and in English literature; he did graduate work in English literature; he taught for a time, as a very young man, and then did a good deal more teaching once his reputation as a writer was established. He was married to three writers; Elizabeth Hardwick, with whom he lived for a quarter of a century, is an immensely intellectual critic of literary and social concerns, as well as a novelist, as is Jean Stafford, Lowell's first wife. (I am not familiar with the work of Caroline Blackwood and can only repeat Axelrod's statement that she is "a gifted writer."[1]) Lowell knew several languages, some of them well; he moved in urban, intellectual circles, where the work of French and Russian and Italian and Spanish and German poets (to name only the languages of the writers in *Imitations*) would be freely and frequently discussed. Lowell's professed desire, accordingly, "to make . . . a small anthology of European poetry," is readily comprehensible.

The trouble, of course, is that alongside that desire, and pretty clearly both a stronger and a more urgent impulse, ran Lowell's need to do at least two other things that neither do nor can square with anthology-making. "This book was written from time to time when I was unable to do anything of my own." Some such inability to write is an exceedingly common phenomenon among writers, and among poets in particular. The wells of poetic creation may run deep, but they do not always run freely. Poets have dry spells, sometimes very long ones: neither the size of the writer's talent nor his accomplishment guarantees against a total inability to write, or at least to compose original work. To cite just one example, Osip E. Mandelstam, one of the greatest poets of this century, was unable to write poetry for a stretch of almost seven years, from 1924 to 1931.[2]

Lowell's problems, as I have cited and discussed them earlier in this book, went considerably deeper, though dry spells were clearly part of what drove him to poems already composed, in other tongues, by other people. It might be argued that Lowell went to those other writers also—and perhaps even primarily—as a calf goes to a cow, or a child to its mother. He needed sustenance: even "help" does not convey the strength and urgency of his need.[3] Many writers—again, chiefly poets—find the resolution of certain craft problems in foreign literatures. When he felt stale and unable to work, Ernest Hemingway would turn to Tolstoy and to *War and Peace* in particular[4]; T. S. Eliot's debt to the French Symbolist poets, and to Jules Laforgue and to Tristan Corbière in particular, is one of the common-places of criticism; Henry James drew heavily on Ivan Turgenev's novels.[5] It could I think be argued that Ezra Pound drew so heavily on writers in languages other than English that, to be sure not for just that reason alone, he ceased to be a truly significant poet in his own language. After reading Eliot's *The Waste Land*, the American poet John Peale Bishop began to study Italian, "so that he could get the full force of the quotations from Dante,"[6] and W. H. Auden correctly observes that "Longfellow had a curiosity about the whole of European literature" compared with which the interest in such matters by Tennyson was insignificant.[7] Lowell's need for help and support, as well as his corresponding uncertainties about his own work, were as I have said especially acute during the time when he produced *Imitations*.

I start, then, with the assumption that Lowell was not what is usually called a translator, and that his book of reworkings from the works of poets writing in other languages is in some sense closer to a volume of original poetry than it is to a volume of translations. But that assumption needs both buttressing and clarification. Indeed, the true nature of *Imitations* cannot I think be perceived except in an analysis of just how its poems differ from true translations. Again, the purpose of this analysis must be to shed light on Lowell as a poet. It is I think necessary to begin with some brief discussion of translation itself, and then to proceed to specific comparisons between a number of the foreign-language originals and what Lowell does (and does not) do with them.

At the minimal level, "Translation is an operation performed on languages: a process of substituting a text in one language for a text in another."[8] At the higher level of literary translation, and specifically verse translation, "One thing seems clear: to translate a poem whole is to compose another poem."[9] Another way of putting it, and here I quote myself, is that "the reader of translations should [not] delude himself that a translation in some way *is* the original. Only the original is the original. . . . "[10] That is, again in my own words,

the kinds of things that you can find in the original, you may or may not find in the translation. You're never going to find exactly the same things. . . . On the minimum level, the linguistic level, the kinds of linguistic phenomena which are manipulated and controlled in one language aren't the same linguistic phenomena which are manipulated and controlled in another language.[11]

Translation thus becomes, willy-nilly, "much more a commentary on the original than a substitute for it."[12] It is of course possible to also argue, faced with such difficulties as these, that translation is impossible. This is essentially the stance taken by Stanley Burnshaw, a fine and knowledgeable critic, who notes that "a verse translation offers an experience in *English* poetry. It takes the reader away from the foreign literature and into his own . . . [but] the instant he departs from the

words of the original, he departs from *its* poetry. For
the words are the poem. Ideas can often be carried
across, but poems are not made of ideas . . . "[13] Burnshaw's solution is to print the original, a plain prose
translation, and an interpretative essay, leaving it to the
reader to recover the original, as best he can, with these
aids. It may well be that poetry is, as Robert Frost
believed, what is lost in translation. "But surely," asks
John Frederick Nims, immediately after quoting this
famous aphorism, "not so lost as poetry in a language we
will never understand? Not quite so lost that there are
no techniques of retrieval?"[14] As even Burnshaw grudg-
ingly admits, "With all its limitations, verse translation
has given us almost all we know of the poets of the rest
of the world."[15]

There is, unfortunately, another response to the
difficulties of literary translation. Vladimir Nabokov,
perhaps its leading exponent, is perfectly forthright
about what he is doing: "In my translation . . . I have
ruthlessly sacrificed manner to matter and have attempted to give a literal rendering of the text as I
understand it."[16] In his version of Pushkin's *Eugene
Onegin*, Nabokov is concerned to make his lines "met-
rically identical"—though this is a linguistic impossibil-
ity—and also to achieve as totally "faithful" a rendering
as possible.[17] Translations done in this fashion are so
abjectly dominated by what linguists call SL, "source
language," that TL, "target language," receives short
shrift indeed.[18] Nabokov's *Eugene Onegin* is barely
readable as English, let alone as poetry. It is in no sense
an adequate presentation, in English, of the great Russian
poem from which it derives. Again, Nabokov and those
who think like him are pursuing a will-o'-the-wisp, an
impossible ideal of "total" or "totally literal" translation.
But as every linguist knows, "Strictly speaking, 'total'
translation is a misleading term, since, though total
replacement is involved it is not replacement by *equiv-*

alents at all levels."[19] "The very shape of thought has to be changed in translation"[20]—or, as John Dryden put it almost three hundred years ago, in attacking the Nabokovians of his day:

The verbal copier is encumbered with so many difficulties at once that he can never disentangle himself from all. He is to consider at the same time the thought of his author, and his words, and to find out the counterpart to each in another language; and, besides this, he is to confine himself to the compass of numbers [i.e., traditional prosody], and the slavery of rhyme. 'Tis much like dancing on ropes with fettered legs: a man may shun a fall by using caution, but the gracefulness of motion is not to be expected; and when we have said the best of it, 'tis but a foolish task; for no sober man would put himself into a danger for the applause of escaping without breaking his neck.[21]

These, then, are the basic critical stances taken toward translation.[22] In applying them to Lowell the critics have been, as I said, neither very sympathetic nor always very perceptive. John Simon, for example, whose orientation is pretty much Nabokovian, entitles his essay on *Imitations* "Abuse of Privilege."[23] The bias of the title is consistent throughout the essay; it leads Simon, as I shall note later in this chapter, to strange and in my view deeply erroneous conclusions about the value of *Imitations*. On the other hand Donald Carne-Ross, whose orientation is clearly anti-Nabokovian, asserts flatly and, as I shall demonstrate, about equally incorrectly, that "Thanks to Robert Lowell, poetic translation retains much of the importance which Ezra Pound won back for it."[24] Again, the bias is both consistent and, in the end, productive of substantially erroneous judgments. Ben Belitt, himself a translator of vast experience, and thus someone who approaches *Imitations* from a practical rather than a theoretical standpoint, comes much closer to the truth of the matter. His essay on the book is entitled "Translation as Personal Mode."[25] I do not think *Imitations* is in fact translation; it definitely is personal.[26]

Lowell's own equipment for attempting the book in the first place was, on the strictly linguistic side, patchy but not insubstantial. His Bachelor of Arts degree was in good part in the classics; his Latin seems to have been good, and he probably knew some but not a great deal of Greek.[27] He spoke of knowing Italian, though on the evidence of *Imitations* he does not seem to me likely to have been fluent in that language.[28] In his own words, "I read French fairly well."[29] "But I know no Russian," he wrote in the Introduction to *Imitations*. He seems to have known not much more German than Russian: in his own slightly contradictory words, on two separate occasions, "I read a lot and stumble away in other languages,"[30] and "I read in the originals, except for Russian."[31] I want to focus on some of the poems drawn from three languages which, as it happens, I myself know more or less as well as Lowell knew them, namely French, Italian, and Russian.[32] Let me take them in that order, and begin with the Renaissance French poet, François Villon (born in 1431; his date of death is not known).

> I am thirty this year,
> near Christmas, the dead season,
> when wolves live off the wind,
> and the poor peasants fear
> the icy firmament.
> Sound in body and mind,
> I write my Testament,
> but the ink has frozen.

Tracking this first stanza of what Lowell calls "The Great Testament" (and which he dedicates to William Carlos Williams) presents some problems. The first line, which is the famous *En l'an de mon trentiesme aage*, is the first line of Villon's "Le Testament." Lines 2 to 5, however, come from the second stanza of "Le Lais"

("The Legacy"), and lines 6 to 8 come partly from the penultimate stanza of "Le Lais" (a poem of 320 lines) and partly from Lowell himself. These licences are freely confessed in the Introduction to *Imitations*: "Villon has been somewhat stripped. . . . Some lines from [his] 'Little Testament' have been shifted to introduce his 'Great Testament.' And so forth! I have dropped lines, moved lines, moved stanzas, changed images and altered meter and intent." His concern, he says, has been not the "literal meaning," which "the usual reliable translator gets," but the "tone," which the "usual reliable translator . . . misses." Since "in poetry tone is of course everything," he explains that "I have been reckless with literal meaning, and labored hard to get the tone." And then he qualifies this statement: "Most often this has been *a* tone, for *the* tone is something that will always more or less escape transference to another language and cultural moment."

Even had Lowell been fully consistent in his dealings with his foreign-language originals, as of course he was not, it would be difficult to extrapolate from just these scant remarks a full-blown theory of translation—or something, at any rate, like translation. All the same, here and elsewhere in his Introduction Lowell does sound more like Stanley Burnshaw than like either Donald Carne-Ross or Vladimir Nabokov. But if as he says "in poetry tone is of course everything," and what he has "labored hard" to achieve is "*a* tone," rather than for the most part "*the* tone," what tone has he fashioned for Villon? Galway Kinnell, the finest translator Villon has had in this century and in our language, has said on this subject: "I have tried to keep the poetry factual, harsh and active, hoping thus to find a tone of voice which might better suit the great original." He speaks too of the "romantic perfume [which] has clung to the English versions of Villon," and emphasizes that "I have tried to resist the literary pressure to play the famous lines and images for all their emotional effect."[33] Kinnell's version of "Le Testament" begins:

> In the time of my thirtieth year
> When I had drunk down all my shames,
> Not all foolish and not all wise
> Despite the many blows I had
> Every one of which I got
> In the clutches of Thibault d'Aussigny . . .

And here is Kinnell's version of the stanza from "Le Lais," from which Lowell has drawn his lines 2 to 5:

> At the time I said above
> Near Christmas, the dead of the year,
> When the wolves live on the wind
> And men stick to their houses
> Against the frost, close by the blaze . . .

Lowell's sixth line, "Sound in body and mind," may be drawn from the third line of the first stanza of "Le Lais," *Considerant, de sens rassis*, which Kinnell translates "Whereas, being sound of mind . . ." Lowell's seventh and eighth lines come largely from a stanza which Kinnell translates like this:

> As soon as my mind was at rest
> And my understanding had cleared
> I tried to finish my task
> But my task was frozen
> And I saw my candle had blown out,
> I couldn't have found any fire,
> So I fell asleep all muffled up
> And couldn't put on a real ending.

It will I think be easier to understand what Lowell has been up to if I set out, very briefly indeed, the general critical consensus about Villon's poetry. Standard critical commentaries tend to emphasize, as does *The Oxford Companion to French Literature*, his "mingled bitterness, melancholy, and humour."[34] Geoffrey Brer-

eton's *A Short History of French Literature* speaks of
his "directness," observing that "while his grossly realistic vein is paralleled in other medieval poets, the
emotional sweep of some of his verse and the bitter
pathos of certain passages are unapproached elsewhere."[35] And Albert Pauphilet, in *Poètes et Romanciers
du Moyen Age*, speaks of Villon's "great theme" as "the
vision of 'these skulls piled up in these charnel-houses',
man's great misery and the bitter consolation of those
who have had no happiness."[36]

How closely does Lowell's version reflect these
comments, and the poet who emerges from Kinnell's
sensitive, "reliable" rendering? To line 4, fairly closely.
Then, when Villon says *Et qu'on se tient en sa maison*,
"And one keeps to one's house," or in Kinnell's version,
"And men stick to their houses," Lowell has "and the
poor peasants fear . . ." There are no peasants at all in
Villon; the notion of "poor" peasants, indeed, seems
very unlikely in his verse, since the only peasants he
would have known were poor. There was no other
variety. A sentimentalizing, even a sensationalizing of
Villon begins to assert itself, at this point. Villon goes
on in the next line to explain that men stay at home
Pour le frimas, pres du tison, "Against the frost, close
by the blaze." Lowell however has his "poor peasants"
in "fear"—which is once again not a Villonesque notion—
and ascribes that fear to "the icy firmament." This is
hardly the "directness," the "bitter pathos," or the gross
realism of which the commentators speak. The last stanza
of "Le Lais," for example, is translated by Kinnell like
this:

> Done on the aforesaid date
> By the very renowned Villon
> Who doesn't eat, shit, or piss,
> Dry and black like a furnace mop
> He doesn't have a tent or pavilion
> That he hasn't left to a friend,

> All he's got is a little change [*peu de billon*]
> That will soon come to an end.

In short, Villon is not the man to worry about an "icy firmament"; his attention is distinctly terrestrial, distinctly unabstract. Donald Carne-Ross enthuses that "Lowell's version of *Le Testament* is, I think, the finest modern account we have of a great medieval poem."[37] Can that really be true, when Lowell has so uncertain a grip on that medieval tone which "is of course everything"?

But it is too soon to formulate a definitive judgment; we need to look farther. The second stanza in Lowell's version, which jumps some two hundred odd lines in "Le Testament," is I think similarly uncertain. Let me set it, for ease of comparison, directly against Kinnell's version:

Lowell:	*Kinnell:*
Where are those gallant men I ran with in my youth?	Where are the happy young men [*gracieux gallans*] Whom I followed in the old days [*temps jadis*]
They sang and spoke so well!	So gifted at singing and talking,
Ah nothing can survive after the last amen; some are perhaps in hell.	So graceful in word and deed?
May they sleep in God's truth;	Some of them are dead and stiff,
God save those still alive!	Nothing remains of them any more,
	May they find rest in Paradise
	And may God save those who are left. [*le remenant*]

Que je suivoye ou temps jadis ("Whom I followed in the old days") is not lexically mangled in Lowell's second line, but is "I ran with" in any way a Villonesque tone? When Pound, who is unfairly blamed for Lowell's

translation excesses, imitated Villon in his "Villonaud"
poems, he was rigorously careful about tone: "Towards
the Noel that morte saison/ *(Christ make the shepherds'*
homage dear!)," or "Drink ye a skoal for the gallows
tree!/ François and Margot and thee and me . . ."[38]
Lowell's third line is also out of key. Villon does not
permit himself such exuberant positiveness—and where
is the wistful flavor (or "tone") of *Si bien chantans, si*
bien parlans ("So gifted at singing and talking")? We
begin to see, too, that Lowell's persona, speaking vi-
brantly of "my youth," is false to Villon's bitter look
backward. *Temps jadis* ("the old days") is aimed backward, and not happily aimed; Lowell's "I ran with in my
youth" is aimed only tangentially backward, its principal
thrust being the sense of pleasure and excitement
experienced. This accounts, too, for the exclamation
mark that Lowell places at the end of line 3. And where
Villon goes on to elaborate, with sober melancholy, on
what has been lost to him (*Si plaisans en faiz et en dis*,
"So graceful in word and deed"), Lowell abruptly inserts
a conclusory "Ah nothing can survive/ after the last
amen." Villon took death a great deal more seriously
than this rather effete sigh. Later in "Le Testament" he
describes (Kinnell's version) *gens mors*, "dead people,"
as "Dead they were body and soul/ In damned perdition,/
Bodies rotted and souls in flames . . . (lines 801–803).
There is no sense of *corps pourris et ames en flammes*
behind Lowell's curiously nineteenth-century line. Nor
would Villon have speculated, twentieth-century style,
that "some are perhaps in hell." *D'eulx n'est il plus riens*
maintenant ("Nothing remains of them any more"), he
says, with true medieval bluntness. So too what he
wishes for the dead is that *Repos aient en paradis* ("May
they find rest in Paradise") which Lowell doubly betrays,
first with "sleep," which seems almost euphemistic here,
and secondly with "in God's truth," more a Puritan than
a Villonesque line. Finally, Lowell's "those still alive"

once more focuses on the positive side of things, the fact
of continued earthly existence, where Villon's emphasis
is on the living's precarious status as *le remenant*.

The examination of Lowell's Villon could be pro-
tracted, but to no purpose. What has been found so far
is what will be found in the rest of it. As Carne-Ross has
also said, rather contradicting himself, Lowell "lacks
Pound's marvellous ability to make new the ancient or
remote."[39] In simple truth, Lowell is oviously unable to
leave the older poetry alone. He insists upon bending
it on his own frame, playing "the famous lines and images
for all their emotional effect"—and then some. Nor,
obviously, is this poetic violence new to Lowell's work
as a whole. "The mimetic brio of his assault upon the
initiating voices [of *Imitations*] is nothing short of ruthless," says Ben Belitt, and "the effect of [*Imitations*] in
the long run is to draw the reader's attention constantly
to the person of the translator, and away from the
ambiance of" those translated.[40]

But Belitt also refers to "the cannibalism of the large
talent at bay,"[41] and the phrase comes very close to a
capsule summary of my argument in this chapter. That
is, why must we look at Lowell's Villon through either
Lowell's *or* Villon's eyes? Why must his Villon-derived
poems be seen either as approximations or as attemped
reflections of the French original? Why not ignore all
questions of *Villon's* tone, "*the* tone," and be content
with Lowell's "The Great Testament" as a separate
poem, influenced by Villon but not dependent upon the
medieval original? Is there, that is, "*a* tone"? Does the
poem work *on its own terms?* I think this last is the
proper question to ask, if not indeed the only question,
for despite all the critical confusion Lowell's "imitations"
seem to me defensible only as "imitations." It simply
will not do to call them translations: you cannot go to
Lowell in order to find Villon. You *can* go to Lowell to
find out how *he* sees Villon—and since Lowell is very

much a "large talent" that vision is an extremely interesting one. It is not strictly speaking either Lowell or
Villon, but it is fine. *Au fort*, says Villon, *quelqu'ung
s'en recompence/ Qui est ramply sur les chantiers/ Car
la dance vient de la pance*. Take me out of the paths of
love, says Villon. "Let someone else make it up, someone
who's filled, right up to the brim, on the loading platforms
at the vineyard, because the dance comes from the
belly." Lowell's version is no version at all, but simply
Lowell's reaction to Villon's version: "Sell love to someone else,/ who puts away more food—/ dancing's for
fatter men!"And whatever we may want to call Lowell's
poem—I happen to think that "imitation" is a perfectly
serviceable term—it is excellent verse. No one confuses
Brahms's Haydn variations with the eighteenth-century
theme and setting that inspired the nineteenth-century
composition. The parallel is by no means exact, and I do
not wish to make any kind of precise analogy. Music is
music, and poetry is poetry, and they are languages far
more alien to one another than are medieval French and
contemporary American English. All the same, some
parallelism does exist. Musical variations tend to be in
the nature of a higher exercise, as are Lowell's imitations.
Musical variations tend to blend the melody and color
of (to borrow the linguists' terms once more) SL and TL,
producing a hybrid not quite like either, but in the final
analysis more like TL than SL. And, though this is
perhaps less clear, musical variations tend as a whole to
be a somewhat slighter form than more strictly original
compositions, tend, that is, to be somewhat less forceful
musical statements.

Nor are we entirely devoid of purely literary ana-
logues. "Imitation," though not quite in Lowell's usage,
was at one time a reognized feature of English literature.
"Come live with me and be my Love," writes Christopher
Marlowe, and Sir Walter Raleigh answers, "If all the
world and love were young," and then John Donne

embroiders in "The Bait," until the once-simple theme is all but buried in his "metaphysical" elaborations. Another and very different aspect of imitation is practiced in the literature of Japan, where revisions of earlier poems, especially the brief and popular form called haiku, are extremely common:

The Japanese poet when expressing his feelings is more likely to use a few words of someone of long ago, words as familiar to everyone in Japan as at one time the famous parts of the Bible were familiar in this country, adding a little and giving to these old words the new accent of the present. It is thus possible in a highly concentrated form to express much to the connoisseur familiar with the allusion, and the change from the old poem needs to be very slight if it is expertly managed.[42]

The form known as linked verse, indeed, is yet another form of imitative literature in Japan. Composed—sometimes orally, spontaneously—by three or sometimes even more persons, the form requires a careful dovetailing of poem after poem to the one just preceding it. The link can be a word, a phrase, an idea, an image; the only requirement is that the connection be neatly, subtly apparent.[43]

Without trying to detail all the examples from the many cultures in which one or more variety of imitation can be found, it seems to me clear that there is a good deal of precedent for considering Lowell's *Imitations* a kind of hybrid form, neither original poetry nor translation, but well worth both producing and reading. I will freely confess that, apart from any and all "translation" questions, *Imitations* seems to me Lowell's most joyful book, tremendous good fun and—significantly—almost lightheartedly cheerful.[44] "I cannot escape the feeling that Lowell translates," speculates John Simon, "when he is unable to write anything of his own, not so much out of love for the poem translated as out of love for the sound of his own poetic voice."[45] The comment is meant to be derogatory, but if we remove the notion

of translation, seeing imitation as a process more like
appreciation, there is I think a good deal of truth in
what Simon says. And if we add, as we must, that
Lowell's voice is a magnificent one, an instrument that
most poets envy and most readers are compelled to
listen to, what can possibly be wrong with it being
exercised? Poets do not turn out poems as short-order
cooks produce pancakes.

We can be less detailed, now, in our tracking of
Lowell's other French-derived poems, as well as in our
tracking of some of his Italian and Russian imitations.
"We would expect him to translate Baudelaire finely,"
says Carne-Ross, "for the two poets have a good deal in
common."[46] I have already noted Carne-Ross's claim that
Lowell achieves a remarkable fidelity, "semantically and
even rhythmically," in his Baudelaire versions. It is an
exaggerated claim, though there is, intermittently, more
Baudelaire in Lowell's Baudelaire than there is Villon
in his Villon. And surely Carne-Ross is right that Lowell
has a good deal in common with Baudelaire. But when
we look closely at the poem Lowell calls "Autumn"—
but which Baudelaire called "Chant d'Automne" ("Song
of Autumn")—we find that it is neither faithful nor
Baudelaire. *Bientôt nous plongerons dans les froides
ténèbres* ("Soon we will plunge into the cold shadows"),
which Lowell renders "Now colder shadows . . . Who'll
turn back the clock?" If Villon's bitter nostalgia did not
appeal to him, neither apparently does Baudelaire's
horrified acceptance of a cold future. *J'entends déjà
tomber avec des chocs funèbres/ Le bois retentissant sur
le pavé des cours*, writes Baudelaire, after a line about
summer's transient *clarté* (clarity, brightness). Lowell
turns this into a line about "bright summer's brief too
lively sport." "Already I hear falling, with funeral ham-
mer-blows,/ timber reverberating on courtyard paving-
stones," one might prosaically render Baudelaire's lines.

Lowell handles the second of these lines brilliantly, but ignores the first: "The squirrel drops its acorn with a shock,/ cord-wood reverberates in my cobbled court." There is no squirrel, and no acorn, in Baudelaire—and I am reminded, not I think irrelevantly, of Tallulah Bankhead, the American actress with a reputation for savage bitchiness, who one day informed an admirer that she had spent the afternoon in the park feeding the squirrels. To her admirer's astonished query, she explained that she had been feeding them to the lions. *That* is true Baudelaire; the sweet squirrel shocked by oncoming winter is not. And again it does not matter, if only we do not expect Lowell's imitation to adequately reflect the original from which it borrows. Taken as the kind of hybrid it in fact is, this first stanza is quite simply masterful:

> Now colder shadows . . . Who'll turn back the clock?
> Goodbye bright summer's brief too lively sport!
> The squirrel drops its acorn with a shock,
> cord-wood reverberates in my cobbled court.

Clearly, Lowell *could* have translated, had that been what he was up to. There are some *aperçus* of vibrant force: "cord-wood" for *le bois* is quite simply gorgeous, and "my cobbled court" for *le pavé des cours* is almost as fine. That however is all the translation there is, unless we take the brutal condensation of "Now colder shadows" as a rendering of *Bientôt nous plongerons dans les froides ténèbres*. But that way lies confusion and empty controversy. As one Charles Caleb Colton said in the 1820s, and others have been repeating ever since. "Imitation is the sincerest form of flattery."[47] "Baudelaire was a real metrist," Lowell said, discussing these versions in an interview. "It was a delight to me just trying to write the quatrains."[48] Why not put aside all notions having to do with translation and simply share that delight?

Interestingly enough, Carne-Ross's strictures on Lowell's imitations of the great Italian poet, Giacomo Leopardi, conclude with much the same judgment that many critics, myself included, have leveled against Lowell's original poetry:

Leopardi, perhaps the last genuinely classical poet Europe has known, writes out of a long literary tradition, intimately known, exactly scrutinized. A single word or phrase ("occhi ridenti") may have behind it the living pressure of five hundred years of literature. No English poetry works in this way; the procedures of modern poetry are wholly different. Lowell, it seems to me, despairing of creating a formal equivalent for Leopardi, and *finding it impossible to work with him, decided to work against him.*[49] [italics mine]

Carne-Ross concludes, accordingly, that "Lowell's versions of Leopardi fail . . . completely,"[50] and John Simon more than agrees, noting that "in the case of such a particularly famous poem [*L'infinito*], the translator's responsibility to the original is even greater than usual."[51] But rather than concluding, as Simon does, that "Lowell's sense of place is faulty," or that he is guilty of "irrelevant Lowellian violence,"[52] I prefer to affirm that Lowell's "The Infinite" is first a poem in its own right and only second "after" Leopardi; it is, again, not a translation at all. Both the gains and the losses can be seen, almost at a glance, by setting Lowell's poem against the translation by Kate Flores:

Flores[53]	*Lowell*
This hidden knoll has always been dear to me,	That hill pushed off by itself was always dear
And this shrubbery, that keeps obscure	to me and the hedges near
So much of the ultimate horizon.	it that cut away so much of the final horizon.
But sitting now and gazing, illimitable	When I would sit there lost in deliberation,
Spaces yonder, and superhuman	I reasoned most on the interminable spaces

Silences, and profoundest
      quiet
Come to mind; where still
      the heart
Knows scarcely fear. And
      listening to the wind
Rustling in this greenery,
      to
That infinite silence I
      compare
This voice: and I ponder
      the eternal,
And the dead seasons, and
      the present
And living, and its sound.
      Thus in this immensity
My meditations drown:
And it is sweet to lose
      myself in this sea.

beyond all hills, on
      their antediluvian
      resignation
and silence that passes
beyond man's
      responsibility.
Here for a little while
      my heart is quiet
      inside me;
and when the wind lifts
      roughing through the
      trees,
I set about comparing my
      silence to those voices,
and I think about the
      eternal, the dead sea-
      sons,
things here at hand
      and alive,
and all their reasons
      and choices.
It's sweet to destroy
      my mind
and go down
and wreck in this sea
      where I drown.

Leopardi's "lyric deeply imbued with philosophical ideas, capable equally of treating themes that are as timeless as they are universal,"[54] frankly does not survive in Mrs. Flores's rendering. "Where still the heart/ Knows scarcely fear," for example, is neither good English nor anything like an adequate rendering of *ove per poco/ Il cor non si spaura* ("where the heart hardly knows fear"). "Illimitable/ Spaces yonder" is a mixture of academic formalism and the speech of the Texas panhandle; "to/ That infinite silence I compare/ This voice" is prosodically so dull that we know, at once, that no first-rate poet could possibly have produced it. In short, Mrs. Flores's version is distinctly minimal translation, giving us some

of the sense but none of the flavor, and above all none
of the impact of the Italian.[55] It is not hard to understand
Carne-Ross's sometimes excessive enthusiasm, comparing the Flores and Lowell poems: "No one can know
how glad I am to find/ On any sheet the least display of
mind," as Robert Frost put it. John Simon, on the other
hand, pursues Lowell past translation and into poetry:

I cannot be wholly unmoved by Propertius' Pound, that is to
say, by what Propertius brought out in Pound. . . . Lowell,
however, is not that free from his models, nor has his free
verse the energy and variety of Pound's. It is the neither-fish-
nor-fowlness of Lowell's imitations, plus all the red herring
they contain, that makes them perverse as translation and
unpalatable as poetry.[56]

It would be my considered judgment, founded on close
study of Pound as a translator, that in fact Lowell's free
verse is, in *Imitations*, frequently (though not always)
superior to Pound's. But Simon is I think doubly wrong,
for Lowell *as a poet* is to my mind a far more significant
figure than Ezra Pound *as a poet*; this is to be sure not
the place to argue the matter. In any event, plainly
Lowell's Leopardi is (to borrow Simon's phrase) really
Leopardi's Lowell; unlike Mrs. Flores's stodgy translation, Lowell's poem is a *poem*. If it is not Leopardi and
it is not strictly speaking Lowell either, so what? If our
categories are at fault, do we need to blame the poet?

"The ten versions from Montale included in *Imitations*," Carne-Ross has said, "constitute by far the most
notable service yet rendered to this great poet in the
English-speaking world."[57] I'm afraid that, considering
these poems as translations, Ben Belitt's judgment is
more accurate: "In comparison with the supple elegance
of Montale, [Lowell's prosody] is peculiarly shrill, prosy,
angular, without reverberations."[58] But compared to the
prosody of even a good "reliable translator," Irma Brandeis, again it is not hard to understand Carne-Ross being
carried away. Here is the opening of *"Notizie
dall'Amiata,"* "News from Amiata," in both versions:

Brandeis[59]
The fireworks of threatening weather
might be murmur of hives at duskfall.
The room has pockmarked beams
and an odor of melons
seeps from the store-room. Soft mists
that climb from a valley
of elves and mushrooms to the diaphanous
    cone
of the crest cloud over my windows
and I write you from here, from this table,
remote, from the honey cell
of a sphere launched into space—
and the covered cages, the hearth
where chestnuts are bursting, the veins
of saltpetre and mould, are the frame
where soon you will break through.

Lowell
Come night,
the ugly weather's fire-cracker simmer
will deepen to the gruff buzz of beehives.
Termites tunnel the public room's rafters to sawdust,
an odor of bruised melons oozes from the floor.
A sick smoke lifts from the elf-huts and funghi of the valley—
like an eagle it climbs our mountain's bald cone,
and soils the windows.
I drag my table to the window,
and write to you—
here on this mountain, in this beehive cell
on the globe rocketed through space.
My letter is a paper hoop.
When I break through it, you will be imprisoned.

Here mildew sprouts like grass from the floor,
the canary cage is hooded with dirty green serge,
chestnuts explode on the grate.

Professor Brandeis, clearly a far more talented translator
than Mrs. Flores, has struggled hard with Montale's

Italian. Lowell has not struggled at all: he has simply
taken what he wanted, changed what he did not; he has
added, he has subtracted. Not that Professor Brandeis
has made no changes: the more talented the translator,
the more apt are there to be changes, the ultimate goal
being a re-creation in the host language (TL). *Le fumate/
morbide*, "delicate smoke," becomes in her version "soft
mists," a romanticization. If Lowell translates the phrase
at all, plainly he mistranslates it as "sick smoke." Were
his a translation, one would be forced to talk of the "false
friend," *morbide*, which is *not* the English word "mor-
bid." Professor Brandeis has chosen to mute *intorbidano*
("to trouble, darken, obscure") in line 8. Apart from the
unfortunate ambiguity of "crest cloud," where "cloud"
might be taken for a noun instead of half the verbal
"cloud over," "cloud over" does not so much reveal as
obscure the force of *intorbidano*. Lowell's "soils the
windows," though it rather stretches the Italian, also
makes it clearer. So too does a great deal of his poem—
that is, it makes *its* images and *its* references clearer
than does Professor Brandeis' translation.

   Lowell's Russian-derived poems, finally, are if anything freer of their originals than are his French and
Italian poems. This is not an insuperable obstacle to
translation; as Carne-Ross says, with considerable authority, "It is desirable, certainly, that the poet-translator
know the language of his original, *but it is not essential*."[60]
However, knowing no Russian has not led Lowell to feel
any more bound by his originals than has the greater
confidence of knowing French or Italian. His "Hamlet
in Russia, A Soliloquy," attributed to Boris Pasternak,
is in fact a collocation and interpretation of three very
different Pasternak poems, no one of which has the title
Lowell uses. His version of Pasternak's "In the Woods"
veers between fairly close tracking of the original and
sudden bursts of theme-and-variations. The first qua-
train, in Lowell's version and in my own (done by
essentially the same procedure), should make clear that,

no matter what the language or what his relationship to it, Lowell's *Imitations* is a pretty consistent performance:

Lowell

A lilac heat sickened the meadow;
high in the wood, a cathedral's sharp, nicked groins.
No skeleton obstructed the bodies—
all was ours, obsequious wax in our fingers ...

Raffel[61]

Meadows blurred in the mauve heat,
in the woods cathedral-darkness expanded.
Was there anything left to kiss?
It was theirs, all of it, soft as warm candles.

And since neither Lowell nor I command the Russian entirely on our own, let me also set out the plain prose translation to be found in *The Penguin Book of Russian Verse:*

> The meadows were blurred by a faintly mauve heat;
> in the wood the darkness of cathedrals swirled.
> What in the world remained for them to kiss?
> It was all theirs, like wax growing soft on their fingers.[62]

(I have taken the liberty of rearranging this prose version in lines comparable to the two verse translations.) Lowell's freedoms, in lines 2 and 3, do not need comment. I trust I may be forgiven, here, if I simply repeat what I have already said, in my book on the translation process, about the differences between Lowell's methods and my own:

It is of course in part a difference in degree: some Old English scholars feel that my [translation of] *Beowulf*, e.g., is a 'free paraphrase' of the original [citation omitted]. The basic difference, I suggest, is that as a *translator* I consider myself bound by the original to a much greater degree than does Lowell when he works as an imitator [citations omitted]. It is my feeling that the difference in degree becomes in truth a difference in kind; Lowell's licenses are consistent, mine occasional.

And this leads to an important further distinction: one does not go to Lowell to find Sappho, Villon, Hugo, and Rilke. Really, I would argue, one almost cannot find them in his pages. It would be an exaggeration to say that there is only one poetic voice in *Imitations*, but it would not be much of an exaggeration.[63]

No one can say—and I suspect that, were he still alive, Lowell himself could not accurately or fully say— what he learned from the intense and on the whole rewarding work that underlay *Imitations*. But freed from the torments of his own subjects, liberated from the responsibility of full creation, Lowell showed a vein of abandon, of gaiety, which does not emerge to anything like this degree anywhere else in his poetry. Able to go his merry way, as it were, unimpeded by his normal exceedingly full measure of constraints and limitations, of memories and pain, of doubts and hesitations, he showed that the poet who began his career with *Land of Unlikeness*, and ended it with *Day by Day*, might some day have united, in a single, overflowing volume of his own poetry, all the strengths and strands to be found, now, spread across the entire body of his work, but never, unfortunately, all in one. Lowell had come a very long way; he had further to go, and the clear hope of making the final leap, when his heart gave out and all further possibility ceased.[64]

6

Half a Step into the Theater

Lowell's connection with the theater is a very real one. Whether he was, as Robert Brustein said in 1965, "a brilliant new dramatist,"[1] is extremely doubtful. Lowell's leaning toward theater and theatrics is in fact exactly that, a leaning, and distinctly peripheral to his major work, which remains his poetry. Indeed, of the eight dramas that Lowell put into print, not one is truly his own. His version of Racine's *Phaedra* (*Phèdre*, in the French) is a translation of sorts, though I would classify it under essentially the same rubric as that discussed in the previous chapter, namely *Imitations*. The three one-act plays published under the collective title, *The Old Glory*, are two of them adapted from stories by Hawthorne, and one adapted from a novella by Melville. His four adaptations from Aeschylus, *Prometheus Bound* and the posthumously published *The Oresteia*, were reworked from other translations—the "dullest I could find," Lowell assures us—and are ruthlessly unlike the Greek original in most respects. "Lowell hoped his version of the Oresteia [w]ould be performed . . . at Lincoln Center," notes Frank Bidart, but "Lincoln Center decided to do Agamemnon alone, in the uncut translation of Edith Hamilton."[2]

Like many poets in the nineteenth century, in short, Lowell felt drawn to the theater, but could not give himself entirely to it. John Simon, much less sympathetic than Robert Brustein, wondered in 1966 if it was still possible to "write truly poetic plays today? The answer, apparently, is no." And he goes on to explain his verdict in words worth reproducing here:

Poetry today has, unfortunately, become a minority art, no longer an integral part of the culture as it was in the heyday of verse drama. Reluctantly, we must accept its divorce from the theater, which must at least *seem* to speak the language of the land. The poet, as writer, may still have a place in the theater; poetry, barring a miracle, does not. What history hath put asunder, no man is likely to join together.[3]

And yet, Lowell did win both awards and praise; his *Phaedra* is I think superbly theatrical writing, and it plays (as I can testify from personal experience) extremely well even in an unstaged reading. And even if Lowell did not become in the strict sense of the word a playwright, his theatrical productions are worth considering both in their own right and for what light they throw on his other and larger achievements.[4]

As I have noted, Lowell's *Phaedra* is much more an imitation than it is a translation; Lowell (like many of his critics) has confused the issue by subtitling the book "a verse translation" (on the cover) and "Racine's Phèdre in an English version" (on the title page), and by referring to himself, in a prefatory note labeled "On Translating *Phèdre*," as unequivocally a translator rather than an imitator. "I have translated as a poet," he says flatly. "My version is *free*, nevertheless I have used every speech in the original, and almost every line is either translated or paraphrased." R. C. Knight, whose heavy-handed scholarly version of the same play appears in the Edinburgh Bilingual Library of European Literature, inevitably dismisses Lowell's version as quite irrelevant: "The word translate I use," he says with some vexation, and not a little snottiness, "in [a] sense . . . which is the opposite of what has lately been done in America by Mr. Robert Lowell."[5] There is no need to look further into the false distinctions already explored in the prior chapter, on *Imitations*. The first seven lines of the play, being Hippolytus's opening speech, in three different versions, should be sufficient to indicate both the futility of the controversy and the nature of Lowell's method:

(1) I have made up my mind, Theramenes.
    No more for me the tranquil days of Trozen,
    For in the mortal tempest of my doubts
    I am dishonoured if I linger here.
    Six months ago my father sailed and left me
    Ignorant what befalls a head so cherished,
    Ignorant even where he may be hidden.[6]

(2) Resolved: I am leaving, dear Theramenes.
    My sojourn in delightful Troezen is ended.
    In this anxiety, this mortal doubt,
    I begin to be ashamed of my idleness.
    More than six months away from my father, I know
    nothing of what befalls so dear a life,
    nor even in what place he may be hidden.[7]

(3) No, no, my friend, we're off! Six months have passed
    since Father heard the ocean howl and cast
    his galley on the Aegean's skull-white froth.
    Listen! The blank sea calls us -- off, off, off!
    I'll follow Father to the fountainhead
    and marsh of hell. We're off. Alive or dead,
    I'll find him.[8]

Versions one and two, both clearly related to a common original (the French, of course, which in this chapter I do not propose to either set out or to discuss), are by Knight and George Dillon, respectively. Mr. Dillon is a poet, and his version, which is plainly a translation, is clearly superior to Knight's (as also, in several places, it is markedly closer to the French). But version three, which is clearly Lowell's, is only vaguely related either to the first two versions or, in point of fact, to the French. Lowell is more than "free." He is violent, and he is far less concerned with what Racine may have

written than what he himself wants to write, starting
with the stimulus of Racine's words. Again, this is
Imitations all over again; it does not seem to me worth
discussing a second time.

But even though Lowell is not translating Racine,
what he does with certain key scenes and speeches is
worth some attention. And it is also worth establishing
from the start that, not only is Racine master of an
"amazing art," to borrow a choice phrase from Lytton
Strachey,[9] but it is pretty generally agreed that the play
Lowell has chosen to work with, *Phèdre*, is "the summit
of Racine's achievement and one of the summits of
European drama."[10] Here then is the young prince
Hippolytus, as close to a hero as this unheroic playwright
is apt to give us, in his early confession to his friend,
Theramenes. Again, I set out the opening lines in three
versions, the first in an older translation by Robert
Henderson, the second in Dillon's version, the third in
Lowell's:

(1) My friend, you must not ask me.
    You who have known my heart through all my
        life,
    And known it to be proud and most disdainful,—
    You will not ask that I should shame myself
    By now disowning all that I professed.
    My mother was an Amazon,—my wildness,
    Which you think strange, I suckled at her breast,
    And as I grew, why, Reason did approve
    What Nature planted in me.[11]

(2)   Dare you say it, friend?
    You who have known my heart since I drew breath,
    can you expect me to deny in shame
    its proud and scornful sentiments? Not only
    was I nourished at the breast of an Amazon
    upon this pride you think astonishing;
    grown to a riper age, I understood
    my own good fortune when I knew myself.

(3)   Theramenes, when I call
        and cry for help, you push me to the wall.
        Why do you plague me, and try to make me fear
        the qualities you taught me to revere?
        I sucked in prudence with my mother's milk.
        Antiope, no harlot draped in silk,
        first hardened me. I was my mother's son
        and not my father's. When the Amazon,
        my mother, was dethroned, my mind approved
        her lessons more than ever. I still loved
        her bristling chastity.

Lowell's own view of the matter is that he has "tried to give my lines a certain dignity, speed, and flare."[12] But what he has done, in simple fact, is turn the grave, distant dignity of Racine's young prince into something very close to the neurotic contrarities of "91 Revere Street," the prose memoir that forms part two of *Life Studies* (and which was, let me note emphatically, written at almost the same time as the *Phaedra* version). Lowell was very much "my mother's son/ and not my father's," as I have indicated. He was also very much a descendant of Puritans, apt to suck in "prudence with my mother's milk." The French, incidentally, specifies not "prudence" but "pride" as what he ingests at his mother's breast (*cet orgueil qui t'étonne*), and the change is in keeping with Lowell's if not with Racine's concerns.

But what happens to a drama predicated upon the cold, unimpassioned nature of Hippolytus, once Hippolytus is reborn as yet another avatar of Robert Lowell, the self-tormenting neurotic *sensitif*? That is, Lowell retains the basic plot structure; people do about what they do in Racine's play; but they act from very different motives. This does more than simply change Racine's *Phèdre*: it transforms and inevitably it weakens it, for Lowell is not enough of a playwright in his own name to accommodate the old plot to the new people and their new motivations. Indeed, not all the motivations are

new; some are essentially as they were, and some are
a mixture of Racine and Lowell, which ultimately sits
uneasily under the old roof. Here, for example, is one
part of Phaedra's confessional scene with her maid,
Oenone, in the third scene of act one, first in Knight's
dogged version and then in Lowell's:

> Oh, I am mad. What have I said?
> Where am I, where are my thoughts,
>   my wandering mind?
> Lost, for the Gods have taken it away.
> My face is hot, Oenone, with my shame;
> I cannot hide my guilty sufferings
> And tears descend that I cannot restrain.

> I have lost my mind.
> Where am I? Oh forget my words! I find
> I've lost the habit now of talking sense.
> My face is red and guilty—evidence
> of treason! I've betrayed my darkest fears,
> Nurse, and my eyes, despite me, fill with tears.

Phaedra emerged from Lowell's lines very much like
Phaedra as Racine created her. But later in the same
scene, when Phaedra declaims magnificently about the
origin of her guilty love for her husband's son, Lowell
intermixes older motivations with some distinctly new
ones. Again, here are first Knight's and then Lowell's
versions:

> It was long ago
> And far from here. When first the rite of Hymen
> Bound my obedience to the son of Aegeus—
> My happiness, my peace then seemed so plain—
> Careless in Athens stood my conqueror.
> I saw and gazed, I blushed and paled again,
> A blind amazement rose and blurred my mind;
> My eyes were dim, my lips forgot to speak,
> This, I knew, was the awful flame of Venus,
> The fated torment of her chosen victims.

My evil comes from farther off. In May,
in brilliant Athens, on my marriage day,
I turned aside for shelter from the smile
of Theseus. Death was frowning in an aisle—
Hippolytus! I saw his face, turned white!
My lost and dazzled eyes saw only night,
capricious burnings flickered through my bleak
abandoned flesh. I could not breathe or speak.
I faced my flaming executioner,
Aphrodite, my mother's murderer!

Lowell does not seem able to understand that height-ening the love-mad queen's torment, and her sensuality, is one thing, while turning an impersonal goddess of love into the murderer of the queen's own mother is something quite else again. To make dramatic sense of the latter is not only impossible, staying as Lowell does within Racine's plot, it is also unthinkable, for the tale of Pasiphae and Minos, Phaedra's mother and father, operates in an entirely different mode and to an entirely different purpose (and the love goddess is not Pasiphae's murderer, for whatever that fact is worth). Lowell's heightening, I think, helps the play he has produced to sound effective, in performance; it does not however help it to make full dramatic sense. But, as I have said, Lowell is not in the full sense a playwright, so the limitation is not particularly important to him. "I have . . . tried to give my lines a certain dignity, speed, and flare," once again, and Lowell is exactly right, that is just what he has tried to do and in good measure has succeeded in doing. But he has been far less concerned with the "diamond-edge" (Lowell's phrase) of Racine's characterizations, and the motivations underlying them. Again, he has "translated," or something like translated, "as a poet"—but not as a dramatist. The difference is both significant and, as I have indicated, pervasive in all his drama-related work.

Indeed, Lowell himself seems pretty clearly to have

recognized the deficiency, in the first of the three one-act plays collected and printed as *The Old Glory,* namely "Endecott and the Red Cross." His note in the revised edition of the play, dated 1968, is as usual somewhat misleading. The play "has been lengthened," he says, "to give it substance, so that it might act by itself . . . What I have added are mostly Indians. Innumerable lines have been 'improved' to be stronger, to be quieter, less in character, more in character." What he has in fact done is add plot, in two principal ways: first, he has added an Indian chief, Assawamsett, who now figures in the first scene and then, after his murder by Endecott, figures in the later scenes both as a narrative impetus and also as a vehicle for better exhibiting Endecott; and second, he has substantially altered the character of Endecott (and the contrasting character of Morton), making him less abstract, better (and more realistically) motivated. The play is indeed much "improved," as are a great many of the lines. Perhaps the single clearest example, in small, is a reference in the first version to "enough solid land/ to drown the sea from here to England," brought back to reality in the revised version as "enough solid land/ to fill up the sea from here to England." The initial image is strained, false, quite worthy of *Land of Unlikeness,* Lowell's contorted first volume of verse. The revised version is indeed "quieter."

But even in the revised version of "Endecott and the Red Cross," there is not enough plot. What John Simon wrote, in 1966, of the original version is still substantially true of the revised version too: "Endecott . . . is an interesting figure who manages to arouse our sympathetic curiosity, but only at the expense of swallowing up most of the playlet: his psyche exacts much more of our attention than do the perfunctory characters and negligible events of the play."[13] Endecott asks one of the "perfunctory characters," a rabid Puritan named Palfrey, "Have you ever seen a hollow suit of armor

walking, or trying to walk?" and goes on to assert,
without any particular reason that we are informed of,
that "I am the hollowness inside my armor." It is well
phrased; it is even psychologically arresting; but it is not
dramatic. We would need to know far more about the
man than that his wife had died in England years before
or that he disliked Archbishop Laud, before we could
truly understand a dramatic impetus at work here. Or
consider the history-lesson-masquerading-as-a-speech,
spruced up in the revised version, but for all that still
a history lesson and abstract, not in any way dramatic:

> England, it is an excellent country,
> if this can be said of a kingdom.
> The Germans gave us gravity and a heart for beer;
> the Normans, cruelty and reason.
> In a hundred fair battles, we have stopped
> the galloping French and headlong Scot.
> We cracked them, then charged them to panic
>   and perdition.
> We have pacified their kingdoms,
> and held them like slaves under our iron prong.
> We have lived through civil wars,
> they were prettily called the Wars of the Roses,
> they were without intention or beauty. . . .

This is perhaps not great poetry, but it is, I would argue,
recognizable at once as poetry, with all the stances and
approaches of a poem. Lowell does not speak to us
through the character, here, or indeed through any
character. The speech is put in the mouth of Endecott;
it could almost as well be assigned to anyone else. Or
to no one else: it is, that is to say, declamation that
matters, here, and not characterization. The speech is
utterly impersonal. But plays are not. Dramatic authors
do not so casually drop into historical moralization—and
I have given only half of this speech, which is renewed
and carried on for some pages still, with interruptions

that are obviously intended to make it more dramatic, but which are rather feeble. Nor do dramatic authors put in the mouths of their characters such lines as, "Remember Michael Wigglesworth's lines on unbaptized children"—and follow this with twenty lines, no less, directly quoted from that colonial poet (1631–1705), who is remembered, if at all, for a long poem of Calvinistic fervor, "The Day of Doom." Early on in the original version, Lowell has Thomas Morton, master of Merry Mount, announce, "I'll read you my new verses," a declaration that the revised version omits, while retaining with very small change the entire poem in question.

And in plain fact the two stories by Hawthorne, "The Maypole of Merry Mount" and "Endicott and the Red Cross," upon which the play draws, are themselves the farthest thing from dramatic. "Had a wanderer, bewildered in the melancholy forest, heard their mirth, and stolen a half-affrighted glance, he might have fancied them the crew of Comus [John Milton's court masque], some already transformed to brutes, some midway between man and beast, and the others rioting in the flow of tipsy jollity that foreran the change. But a band of Puritans, who watched the scene, invisible themselves, compared the masque to those devils and ruined souls with whom their superstition peopled the black wilderness."[14] We do not remember Hawthorne for stories so inert and stiffly written as this. When Robert Brustein claims, in the introductory essay to the original printing of *The Old Glory* (his essay has been dropped from the revised version), that "Mr. Lowell has managed to adapt these tales with relative fidelity to the original texts," the claim is neither accurate nor meaningful. It is impossible to say, in the absence of some express declaration from Lowell himself, just why he was drawn to fiction so pallid, static, and ideational. Most adapters of other people's stories feel the tug of a striking character, a striking setting, a striking chain of events.

Lowell apparently felt the tug of an idea—and that fact is surely significant.

"My Kinsman, Major Molineux," the second of the three plays in *The Old Glory*, draws upon yet another Hawthorne tale of this same name. It is a wonderfully dramatic story, one of Hawthorne's best, with a powerful narrative urge and a number of vivid characterizations, and with an ending that has all of the surprise but much more than the force of a typical O'Henry tale. The play's first director, Jonathan Miller, writes in a "Director's note" to the original edition that *"My Kinsman, Major Molineux* is the most stylized of the three plays and it needs to be put across with scintillating artificiality." John Simon puts it more brutally: "In *Molineux*, the absurdist mode is fairly consistent (though not so witty as in Beckett or Ionesco), but it clashes with stabs at mythologizing . . . and, throughout, one feels a certain confusion between symbol and rigmarole."[15] And yet, oddly, though strongly unlike the Hawthorne tale, and for all its rather glaring inanities, "My Kinsman, Major Molineux" is both more dramatic and more original than "Endecott and the Red Cross." Had Lowell been able to resist the pretentious, heavy-handed "mythologizing" that Simon speaks of and focus instead on the "scintillating artificiality" which, at moments, he does beautifully, the play would have been vastly improved. In the play's first minute the ferryman who takes Robin, the main character, across the river to Boston proclaims solemnly, "No one returns"—and we have small doubt that we are in for it, dose after dose of archness and intellectualized humor. There is a good deal of that. After a meeting with a prostitute, Robin declares "I wish I knew the naked truth"; meeting with a Man with a Mask, who talks in circles, Robin says, embarrassingly, "You talk like Christ," and then tells his younger brother (an invention of Lowell's, called with flatfooted simplicity, "Boy") that "He is someone out of 'Revelations'—

Hell revolting on its jailers." But there is also a good
deal of pageantlike writing that works dramatically. "My
Kinsman, Major Molineux" is a slender strand on which
to credit Lowell with genuine dramatic talent, but signs
of that talent do show, no matter how confused.

Benito Cereno is one of Melville's powerful, con-
densed late tales, a story of great suspense and ingen-
iously worked-out detail. Lowell keeps the main outline
of the story, but consistently oversimplifies; surrendering
realistic detail and adding some very gaudy touches, he
manages not to heighten but to lessen the story's impact.
Curiously, along with a Hollywoodlike concept of action
as cops-and-robbers stuff and the invention of a first
mate, Perkins, of totally cardboard dimensions, Lowell
also practices an intermittent poeticism that is both
distracting and deeply undramatic. Spotting the Spanish
ship, for example, the American captain looks through
his telescope and reports what he sees in superheated
irrelevancies:

> I see an ocean undulating in long scoops of swells;
> it's set like the beheaded French Queen's high wig;
> the sleek surface is like waved lead,
> cooled and pressed in the smelter's mould.
> I see flights of hurried gray fowl,
> patches of fluffy fog.
> They skim low and fitfully above the decks,
> like swallows sabering flies before a storm.
> This gray boat foreshadows something wrong.

The last line of this nine-line speech is the only one that
approaches dramatic utility; the rest is, like Lowell's fog,
mere fluff. Nor does the captain stop at this, going on
in other speeches to describe the Spanish ship in very
similar, equally irrelevant terms. Indeed, where Melville
gives the American captain a disjointed, half terrified,
totally neurasthenic recollection of his childhood days
on the beach, ending with "Fie, fie . . . you are a child
indeed; a child of the second childhood, old boy; you are

beginning to dote and drool, I'm afraid," Lowell leans
on the passage, making it both consecutive and poetic—
and thereby rendering it dramatically inert:

> Carrying a duck-satchel in my hand, I used to paddle
> along the waterfront from a hulk to school.
> I didn't learn much there. I was always shooting duck
> or gathering huckleberries along the marsh with Cousin
> Nat!
> I like [?] nothing better than breaking myself on the surf.
> I used to track the seagulls down the five-mile stretch of
> beach for eggs.
> How can I be killed now at the ends of the earth
> by this insane Spaniard?
> Who could want to murder Amasa Delano?
> My conscience is clean. God is good.
> What am I doing on board this nigger-pirate ship?

There are good things in Lowell's "Benito Cereno,"
craftsmanlike touches that exhibit, as in "My Kinsman,
Major Molineux," a streak of genuine dramatic ability.
But they are relatively few and relatively far between.
Robert Brustein asserts, I think very wrongly, that the
play "has all the theatrical power of the first two [*Old
Glory*] plays, as well as a heavily charged prose style
and a strong suspenseful narrative."[16] John Simon, it
seems to me, hits very much closer to the mark:

And it is true of all three plays that, though they are aware of
the things that make a play a play—not merely action and
conflict, as commonly held, but also diversified verbal texture,
humor, pathos, variety of tempo, absorbing talk, and so on—
he is unable either to provide enough of them or to marshal
them properly.[17]

Lowell's four adaptations from Aeschylus, *Prometheus Bound* and the three plays which comprise *The
Oresteia*, are as I have said ruthlessly unlike the Greek
originals in most respects. "Half my lines are not in the
original," Lowell notes in his brief prefatory remarks to
Prometheus Bound. "Using prose instead of verse, I was

free to tone down the poetic eloquence, and *shove in*
any thought that occurred to me and seemed to fit"
[italics mine]. There is a casually brutal attitude toward
the originals, here, which seems to me to go far beyond
what Lowell practiced in *Imitations*. In the *Oresteia*
plays, indeed, Lowell couples this with a compression
so fierce that virtually nothing of the original remains.
His *Agamemnon* occupies forty-seven heavily-leaded
pages, with a maximum of about thirty lines to a page.
His *Orestes* (*The Libation Bearers*) has thirty-eight
pages, similarly set; his *The Furies* (*Eumenides*) has
barely thirty. In the Greek *Agamemnon* has just under
1,700 lines, *The Libation Bearers* has 1,075, and *Eumenides* has 1,090. Lowell's versions have, in short,
about 1,000 lines fewer than the Greek. Nor is it simply
a matter of compression in number of lines, for Lowell
is far more ruthless than that. Here for example is the
watchman's speech, when he sees the light signaling the
end of the Trojan War, first in Richmond Lattimore's
translation, and then as presented by Lowell:

> Oh hail, blaze of the darkness, harbinger of day's
> shining, and processionals and dance and choirs
> of multitudes in Argos for this day of grace.
> Ahoy!
> I cry the news aloud to Agamemnon's queen,
> that she may rise up from her bed of state with speed
> to raise the rumor of gladness welcoming this beacon,
> and singing rise, if truly the citadel of Ilium
> has fallen, as the shining of this flare proclaims.
> I also, I, will make my choral prelude, since
> my lord's dice cast aright are counted as my own,
> and mine the tripled sixes of this torchlit throw.

> What am I seeing? The sky's on fire.
> I must run and call the Queen.
> There'll be shouting and dancing in the streets.
> She will lead the dancers through Argos.
> Troy's down, Troy's burning!
> The dice have fallen right for my King.

What David Ignatow, a poet of Lowell's generation but of very different styles and concerns, has said of Lowell's own poetry, necessarily with some degree of unfairness, seems to me perfectly fair when applied to work of this sort. Lowell, Ignatow asserts, did not take his life "seriously enough" or see it "in its tragic context. There's a sense of distaste in Lowell's work, a kind of disdain for his life—a weariness with it. . . . [He has] a contempt for [his] material."[18] Let me contrast what we have seen, even in this brief passage, Lowell doing to Aeschylus with the following sober, accurate, professional, and immensely respectful judgment: "The *Oresteia* is Aeschylus' acknowledged masterpiece in every dramatic element . . . the culmination of Aeschylus' dramaturgy . . . [possessing] such enormous sweep and power that we lesser mortals ought to criticize . . . , if criticize . . . we must, on our knees."[19] There is no need for Robert Lowell to have gone on his knees to anyone, Aeschylus included. But neither was it necessary for him to treat plays of such commanding stature as objects into which he "was free . . . to shove in any thought that occurred to me and seemed to fit." I feel obliged to conclude, and to conclude this book, by noting how very typical of Robert Lowell—in his poetry, in his so-called translations, and to a large extent also in his personal life—such an extraordinary act of licence in fact was. I do not think it is really accurate to say that he had "a contempt for [his] material." Rather, I would say, he had a kind of whirling contempt that oscillated between himself and his world, between himself and other human beings. It did not operate at all times and in all things, nor did it disable him. But it sometimes crippled him, and sometimes it crippled his poetry, and as I think it is very clear, to my mind, it totally unfitted him in his dealings with Aeschylus.

Notes

1.   FROM BOSTON TO NEW YORK:
A SKETCH OF LIFE AND WORK

1. Steven Gould Axelrod, *Robert Lowell, Life and Art* (Princeton: Princeton University Press, paperback, 1979), p. 75.
2. Quoted from Axelrod, p. 74.
3. Elizabeth Hardwick, *A View of My Own, Essays in Literature and Society* (New York: Farrar, Strauss, Noonday paperback, 1963), pp. 95, 100.
4. Axelrod, p. 92.
5. Richard Howard, "Fuel on the Fire," quoted from Michael London and Robert Boyers, eds., *Robert Lowell: A Portrait of the Artist in His Time* (New York: David Lewis, 1970), pp. 98, 99.
6. R. K. Meiners, *Everything to be Endured, An Essay on Robert Lowell and Modern Poetry* (Columbia: University of Missouri Press, 1970), p. 48.

2.   A STRAINED START, A PULITZER PRIZE, AND A
CONFUSED CONTINUATION: THE FIRST THREE BOOKS

1. In the preface to his *Essays of Four Decades* (Chicago: Swallow Press, 1968), p. xi, by way of explanation of his own literary contexts, Tate says forthrightly that "What I owe to T. S. Eliot is pervasive. . . . [He was] a model of what the non-academic man of letters ought to be."
2. T. S. Eliot, *For Lancelot Andrewes: Essay on Style and Order* (London: Faber and Faber, 1928), p. ix.
3. T. S. Eliot, "The Metaphysical Poets," in *Selected Essays of T. S. Eliot* (New York: Harcourt, Brace, 1950), p. 247.
4. R. P. Blackmur, "Notes on Seven Poets," in *Form and*

Value in Modern Poetry (Garden City: Anchor paperback, 1957), p. 335.

5. Hayden Carruth, "A Meaning of Robert Lowell," in London and Boyers, p. 231.

6. In my essay-review, "In Gloom Embowering Beyond the Glade," *Michigan Quarterly Review* XIX (1980): 253, 256, I have said of Tate that he "is constantly trying to write Literature, that he is far more comfortable with poems than with people and events. . . . Even at his generally accepted best, he is stale, derivative, and fatally self-conscious . . . endlessly verbal and almost never real."

7. Randall Jarrell, "Fifty Years of American Poetry," *The Third Book of Criticism* (New York: Farrar, Straus & Giroux, 1969), p. 332.

8. William Arrowsmith, "A Monotony of Violence," in London and Boyers, p. 35.

9. Blackmur, p. 335.

10. Marius Bewley, "From *The Complex Fate*," in London and Boyers, p. 9.

11. Axelrod, p. 50.

12. Carruth, in London and Boyers, p. 227.

13. Will C. Jumper, "Whom Seek Ye? A Note on Robert Lowell's Poetry," in Thomas Parkinson, ed., *Robert Lowell : A Collection of Critical Essays* (Englewood Cliffs: Prentice-Hall, 1968), p. 53.

14. Randall Jarrell, "From the Kingdom of Necessity," in London and Boyers, p. 27.

15. *The Collected Poems of Weldon Kees*, ed. Donald Justice (Lincoln: University of Nebraska Press, 1962), p. 109–10.

16. Axelrod, p. 53.

17. See, e.g., John Bayley, "Robert Lowell: The Poetry of Cancellation," in London and Boyers, p. 187.

18. Jerome Mazzaro, *The Poetic Themes of Robert Lowell* (Ann Arbor: University of Michigan Press, 1965), p. 37. Mazzaro, who is also the leading bibliographer in Lowell studies, offers without question the best discussion of the poet's intellectual concerns and their sources.

19. Axelrod, p. 63.

20. Irvin Ehrenpreis, "The Age of Lowell," in London and Boyers, p. 170.

21. Randall Jarrell, "The Mills of the Kavanaughs," in London and Boyers, p. 40.

22. "Wallace Stevens' 'Sunday Morning'," says Axelod, p. 184, is "a poem that had haunted Lowell's imagination ever since he repeatedly copied it into his notebooks at Kenyon College."

23. Randall Jarrell, "The Mills of the Kavanaughs," in London and Boyers, p. 42.

24. Mazzaro, p. 84.

3. PLUGGING INTO LIFE; THE PLUG REFUSES TO HOLD:
Life Studies AND AFTER.

1. M. L. Rosenthal, "Robert Lowell and the Poetry of Confession," in London and Boyers, p. 49.

2. Norman Mailer, "From *The Steps of the Pentagon*," in London and Boyers, p. 243.

3. Robert Lowell, "On 'Skunk Hour'," in *Robert Lowell: A Collection of Critical Essays*, ed. Thomas Parkinson, pp. 132–33.

4. Interview, in London and Boyers, pp. 268–69.

5. Ezra Pound, "The Prose Tradition in Verse," *Literary Essay of Ezra Pound*, ed. T. S. Eliot (London: Faber and Faber, 1954), p. 377. See Ehrenpreis, in London and Boyers, p. 173, and Mazzaro, p. 89. And see too Frederick Seidel's introduction to the Interview, London and Boyers, p. 261, which begins: "On one wall of Mr. Lowell's study was a large portrait of Ezra Pound . . ."

6. London and Boyers, p. 270.

7. Axelrod, pp. 108–09.

8. I think it ought to be said, however, that when *Life Studies* appeared Schwartz was just publishing his well-received *Summer Knowledge*. His artistic promise had already dimmed, surely, and among those acquainted with him it was common knowledge that his mental state was problematical. (But then, so too was Lowell's.) The

situation was by no means hopeless, accordingly, when
Lowell produced and then published this poem, and it
should not be read as the sort of final elegy that later
events might well have inspired.

9. Interview, *Delos* I (1968): 166.

10. For a much fuller analysis of the poems of part four, see
    my essay, "Robert Lowell's *Life Studies*," *The Literary
    Review* XXIII (1980): 293–325.

11. Parkinson, pp. 124–30 and 131–34.

12. See Anthony Ostroff, ed., *The Contemporary Poet as
    Artist and Critic* (Boston: Little Brown, 1964).

13. Richard J. Fein, "The Life of *Life Studies*," *The Literary
    Review* XXIII (1980): 326–38. And for basic reading of
    the poem—its references, its geography—see John V.
    Hagopian, "Robert Lowell's *Skunk Hour*," in *Insight III:
    Analyses of English and American Poetry*, ed. Reinhold
    Schiffer and Herman J. Weiand (Frankfurt: Hirschgraben
    Verlag, 1969), pp. 170–80.

14. The poem that took over the final slot, titled in this early
    appearance "Colonel Shaw and the Massachusetts 54th,"
    was to become, retitled, the final, weightiest, and now
    also the title poem of his next book, *For the Union Dead*.
    I will discuss it as part of that later volume rather than
    as a part of *Life Studies*.

15. Helen Vendler, *Part of Nature, Part of Us* (Cambridge:
    Harvard University Press, 1980), p. 133. The best essay
    on *For the Union Dead* that I have ever seen is Thomas
    Parkinson, "For the Union Dead," in Parkinson, pp.
    143–51.

16. For a useful discussion, subtitled "Starting Over: Learning
    from Williams," see Axelrod, pp. 84–101.

17. I do not think Lowell does nearly as well, in adding an
    intrusive, sonnet-style stanza to a poem from *Life Studies*,
    "Beyond the Alps." This reworking of finished (and
    published) poems is of course a special kind of restlessness
    of its own. Significantly, one of the relatively few other
    poets who displays it is Lowell's early mentor, Allen Tate.

18. This, to be sure, has been noted before—for example, by
    Axelrod, p. 174.

19. Axelrod, p. 173.

20. Meiners, p. 61.
21. Meiners, p. 63.

4. PROLIFIC MEDIOCRITY AND A FINAL TRIUMPH: EVERYTHING ENDS WITH *Day by Day*

1. The two primary "dream song" books are 77 *Dream Songs* (New York: Farrar, Straus and Giroux, 1964), and *His Toy, His Dream, His Rest* (New York: Farrar, Straus and Giroux, 1968).
2. Axelrod, p. 206.
3. Vendler, p. 126.
4. Axelrod, p. 212.
5. Axelrod, p. 213.
6. Vendler, p. 165. She is writing, of course, about *Day by Day* as well as the other late volumes, and as to that final book I am in almost total agreement with her, as the concluding pages of this chapter will show.
7. Vendler, pp. 125, 133.
8. Vendler, pp. 172–73.
9. Lowell's rhymes, William Carlos Williams once said, are something he forces himself into—because "He must, to his mind, appear to surmount them." William Carlos Williams, "In a Mood of Tragedy: *The Mills of the Kavanaughs*," in London and Boyers, p. 36.
10. As a poet and a teacher of poets, I cannot help pointing out that Lowell tended all his life to over-punctuate, and in particular to end a line clearly meant to be enjambed with a cluttering, interfering (and apparently automatic) comma. The first line, here, is I think a clear example. In reading Lowell aloud these commas should be, in my judgment, ignored.
11. Vendler, p. 164.

5. PICKING PEBBLES OUT OF FOREIGN SAND: *Imitations*

1. Axelrod, p. 214.
2. Sidney Monas, "Introduction," *Complete Poetry of Osip*

Emilevich Mandelstam, trans. Burton Raffel and All Burago (Albany: State University of New York Press, 1973), p. 15. See also Clarence Brown, *Mandelstam* (Cambridge: Cambridge University Press, 1973), pp. 121 ff.

3. " . . . Robert Lowell clearly presents a special study. He is the first important poet to take an explicitly psychoanalytical view of his own history . . . Lowell's habits of mind are intrinsically psychological . . . " Alan Williamson, *Pity the Monsters: The Political Vision of Robert Lowell* (New Haven: Yale University Press, 1974), p. 5. Williamson's is a book with which I am for the most part out of sympathy; it is however so intelligently written, and so closely argued, that a reader of any point of view will find provocative and useful things in its pages.

4. "Tolstoi made the writing of Stephen Crane on the Civil War seem like the brilliant imagining of a sick boy who had never seen war but had only read the battles and chronicles and seen the Brady photographs . . . " Ernest Hemingway, *A Moveable Feast* (New York: Bantam paperback, 1965), p. 132.

5. "George Moore once remarked that Henry James went abroad and read Turgenev while William Dean Howells stayed at home and read Henry James." Leon Edel, *Henry James, The Untried Years: 1843–1870* (Philadelphia: Lippincott, 1953), p. 275.

6. Charles Norman, E. E. Cummings, *The Magic Maker* (Boston: Little, Brown paperback, 1972), p. 151.

7. W. H. Auden, *The Dyer's Hand* (New York: Random House, 1962), p. 355. Auden adds, neatly: "Even if there had been Red Indians roaming the North of Scotland, . . . one cannot imagine Tennyson sitting down to write a long poem about them and choosing for it a Finnish meter"—as Longfellow indeed did, for *Hiawatha.*

8. J. C. Catford, *A Linguistic Theory of Translation* (London: Oxford University Press, 1965), p. 1.

9. Jackson Mathews, "Third Thoughts on Translating Poetry," in Reuben A. Brower, ed., *On Translation* (New York: Oxford University Press paperback, 1966), p. 67.

10. Burton Raffel, *The Forked Tongue, A Study of the Translation Process* (The Hague: Mouton, 1971), p. 19.

11. *Why Re-Create? A Conversation about Translations with Burton Raffel, conducted by Vincent J. Cleary* (San Francisco: Chandler and Sharp, 1973), p. 13.

12. Donald Carne-Ross, "Translation and Transposition," in William Arrowsmith and Roger Shattuck, eds., *The Craft and Context of Translation* (Austin: University of Texas Press, 1961), p. 6.

13. Stanley Burnshaw, *The Poem Itself* (New York: Holt, Rinehart and Winston, 1960), pp. xi–xii.

14. John Frederick Nims, *Sappho to Valery: Poems in Translation* (New Brunswick: Rutgers University Press, 1971), p. 1.

15. Nims, p. xiii.

16. *The Story of Igor's Campaign*, trans. Vladimir Nabokov (New York: Vintage paperback, 1960), p. 17.

17. Vladimir Nabokov, *Notes on Prosody* (New York: Pantheon paperback, 1964), p. 46 and *passim*.

18. See Catford, *passim*.

19. Catford, p. 22.

20. Edwin and Willa Muir, "Translating from the German," in Brower, p. 94.

21. John Dryden, *Of Dramatic Poesy and Other Critical Essays*, ed. G. Watson (London: Everyman's Library, 1962), I, 269. These words were written in 1680.

22. See *The Forked Tongue*, pp. 12–13, n. 4, where I have also largely summed up my own view, in this more or less technical argument, by noting that, while Lowell "is doing interesting work," what he is "practising, however, is cultural diffusion, not translation." I rather doubt that the technical argument is relevant, here; I cite these words of mine chiefly to indicate that different discussions require different levels of discourse, and may sometimes also require different conclusions.

23. John Simon, "Abuse of Privilege: Lowell as Translator," in London and Boyers, pp. 130–151.

24. Interview, *Delos* I (1968): 165. In his essay, "The Two Voices of Translation," in Parkinson, pp. 152–70, Carne-Ross gets sufficiently carried away to assert, on the whole

quite wrongly, that "what is remarkable about Lowell's versions from Baudelaire is that they stick so closely to the original, semantically and even rhythmically . . . " (p. 161).

25. London and Boyers, pp. 115–29.
26. Says Belitt, "The effect . . . is to draw the reader's attention constantly to the person of the translator . . . ." P. 115.
27. "He knows a little Greek, but I imagine that he prefers to work mainly with prose versions." Carne-Ross, in Parkinson, p. 157.
28. Interview, *Delos* I (1968): 167.
29. Interview, *Delos* I (1968): 168.
30. Interview, *Delos* I (1968): 171.
31. London and Boyers, p. 280.
32. For the record, my French is probably better, my Italian less good; I know some but by no means enough Russian.
33. Francois Villon, *The Poems of Francois Villon*, trans. Galway Kinnell (New York: Signet paperback, 1965), p. 19. I prefer this to the more recent *The Poems of Francois Villon* (Boston: Houghton Mifflin, 1977). All quoted passages from Kinnell's translations of Villon, accordingly, are from the earlier book. And since further these passages are easily locatable, I have not cluttered my text with unnecessary footnote citations.
34. *The Oxford Companion to French Literature*, ed. P. Harvey and J. E. Heseltine (Oxford: Oxford University Press, 1959), p. 749.
35. Geoffrey Brereton, *A Short History of French Literature* (Harmondsworth: Penguin paperback, 1954), pp. 34, 36.
36. *Poetes et Romanciers du Moyen Age*, ed. Albert Pauphilet (Paris: Gallimard, 1952), p. 1134. The translation here is my own.
37. Parkinson, p. 159.
38. Ezra Pound, "Villonaud for this Yule" and "A Villonaud: Ballad of the Gibbet," *Personae* (New York: New Directions, n.d.), pp. 10, 11.
39. Parkinson, p. 159.
40. London and Boyers, pp. 116, 115.
41. London and Boyers, p. 117.

42. Donald Keene, *Japanese Literature* (New York: Grove paperback, 1955), p. 30.

43. Keene, p. 31–37.

44. "Two of the poems by Rimbaud are splendidly joyous," says Louis Simpson in "Matters of Tact," London and Boyers p. 113.

45. Simon, "Abuse of Privilege," London and Boyers, pp. 136–37. I am assuming that what Simon in fact wrote is "the sound of his own poetic voice," though as printed he is made to say, I suspect wrongly, "the sound of his own poetic vice."

46. Parkinson, p. 160.

47. In his two-volume *Lacon* (1820–1822). Colton is described in *Chamber's Biographical Dictionary* (Edinburgh: W. & R. Chambers, 1961), p. 299, as a "clergyman, sportsman, gambler, suicide and author . . . "

48. Interview, *Delos* I (1968): 169.

49. Donald Carne-Ross, in Parkinson, p. 165.

50. Carne-Ross, in Parkinson, p. 166.

51. Simon, "Abuse of Privilege," London and Boyers, p. 139.

52. Simon, "Abuse of Privilege," London and Boyers, pp. 139, 140.

53. In Giacomo Leopardi, *Leopardi: Poems and Prose,* ed. Sergio Pacifici (Bloomington: University of Indiana Press, 1966), p. 61.

54. Leopardi, pp. 10–11.

55. "When translations from one language into another are undertaken the task must be entrusted to one who is a creative writer in that particular genre (novel, short-story, play, *etc.*), as such a person alone can rightly understand and assess the significance of the situations, characters and dialogue. Translations assigned to mere scholars often turn out to be arid, heavy stuff." Pothukuchi Suryanarayana Murty, book review, *The Indian P.E.N.* XXX (July 1964): 226.

56. Simon, "Abuse of Privilege," London and Boyers, pp. 143–44.

57. Parkinson, p. 166.

58. London and Boyers, p. 123.

59. Eugenio Montale, *Selected Poems,* ed. Glauco Cambon (New York: New Directions, 1965), pp. 83, 85.

60. Parkinson, p.157.

61. Burton Raffel, *Russian Poetry Under the Tsars* (Albany: State University of New York Press, 1971), p. 233.

62. *The Penguin Book of Russian verse,* ed. Dimitri Obolensky (Harmondsworth: Penguin paperback, 1962), p. 332.

63. Raffel, *The Forked Tongue,* p. 102 n. 8

64. Portions of this chapter are founded on, and revised from, my essay, "Robert Lowell's *Imitations,*" *Translation Review* #5 (Summer, 1980): 20–27.

6. HALF A STEP INTO THE THEATER

1. Robert Brustein, "The Old Glory," in London and Boyers, p. 79.

2. Frank Bidart, "Note on the Text," in Robert Lowell, *The Oresteia* (New York: Farrar, Straus & Giroux paperback, 1978), n.p.

3 John Simon, "Strange Devices on the Banner," in London and Boyers, p. 83.

4. " . . . almost from the beginning, he has sought to fulfill an epic ambition with essentially lyric means," writes Stephen Yenser, with the sensitive acuity typical of his study of Lowell, *Circle to Circle* (Berkeley: University of California Press, 1975), p. 298. I think Yenser sees far more structure in Lowell's work, volume by volume, than in fact exists. But his detailed analyses of the poetry are among the best yet to see print.

5. Jean Racine, *Phèdre,* ed. and trans. R. C. Knight (Austin: University of Texas Press, 1971), p. 15.

6. Knight, p. 31.

7. Jean Racine, *Three Plays of Racine,* trans. George Dillon (Chicago: University of Chicago Press paperback, 1961), p. 127.

8. Robert Lowell, *Racine's Phaedra* (New York: Farrar, Straus and Giroux paperback, 1961), p. 11.

9. Lytton Strachey, "Racine," in *Literary Essays* (New York: Harcourt, Brace paperback, n.d.), p. 66.

10. Martin Turnell, *Jean Racine—Dramatist* (New York: New Directions, 1972), p. 239.
11. *Six Plays by Corneille and Racine*, ed. Paul Landis (New York: Modern Library, 1931), p. 251.
12. Robert Lowell, *Phaedra*, p. 8.
13. Simon, "Strange Devices," p. 81.
14. *The Complete Novels and Selected Tales of Nathaniel Hawthorne*, ed. Norman Holmes Pearson (New York: Modern Library, 1937), p. 883.
15. Simon, "Strange Devices," p. 81.
16. Brustein, "The Old Glory," p. 78.
17. Simon, "Strange Devices," p. 82.
18. David Ignatow, *Open Between Us* (Ann Arbor: University of Michigan Press paperback, 1980), pp. 149–50.
19. Gerald F. Else, *The Origin and Early Form of Greek Tragedy* (Cambridge: Harvard University Press, 1965), p. 100.

Bibliography

1. WORKS BY LOWELL

Poetry: original

Land of Unlikeness. Cummington, Mass.: Cummington Press, 1944.

Lord Weary's Castle. New York: Harcourt, Brace, 1946.

Poems: 1938–49. London: Faber & Faber, 1950.

The Mills of the Kavanaughs. New York: Harcourt, Brace, 1951.

Life Studies. New York: Farrar, Straus, 1959.

For the Union Dead. New York, Farrar, Straus, 1964.

Selected Poems. London: Faber, & Faber, 1965.

Near the Ocean. New York: Farrar, Straus, 1967.

Notebook 1967–1968. New York: Farrar, Straus, 1969.

Notebook, rev. ed. New York: Farrar, Straus, 1970.

The Dolphin. New York: Farrar, Straus, 1973.

For Lizzie and Harriet. New York: Farrar, Straus, 1973.

History. New York: Farrar, Straus, 1973.

Selected Poems. London: Faber & Faber, 1976.

Day by Day. New York: Farrar, Straus, 1977.

Poetry: from other languages

Imitations. New York: Farrar, Straus, 1961.

'The Voyage' and Other Versions of Poems by Baudelaire. New York: Farrar, Straus, 1968.

Dramatic Adaptations

Racine's Phaedra. New York: Farrar, Straus, 1961.

The Old Glory. New York: Farrar, Straus, 1964.

The Old Glory, rev. ed. New York: Farrar, Straus, 1968.

Prometheus Bound. New York: Farrar, Straus, 1969.
The Oresteia. New York: Farrar, Straus, 1978.

Prose Writings

There is no collection. Yenser, pp. 352–53, lists virtually
everything of interest.

2. WORKS ABOUT LOWELL

Bibliographies

Mazzaro, Jerome, *The Achievement of Robert Lowell: 1939–59*.
Detroit: University of Detroit Press, 1960.
———, "A Checklist of Materials on Robert Lowell: 1939–68,"
in London and Boyers.
Staples, Hugh B., Appendix II, in *Robert Lowell: The First
Twenty Years*. New York: Farrar, Straus, 1962.

Criticism

BOOKS

Axelrod, Steven Gould, *Robert Lowell, Life and Art*. Princeton:
Princeton University Press paperback, 1979.
Fein, Richard J., *Robert Lowell*. New York: Twayne, 1970.
London, Michael and Robert Boyers, eds., *Robert Lowell: A
Portrait of the Artist in His Time*. New York: David Lewis,
1970.
Mazzaro, Jerome, *The Poetic Themes of Robert Lowell*. Ann
Arbor: University of Michigan Press, 1965.
Meiners, R. K., *Everything To Be Endured: An Essay on
Robert Lowell and Modern Poetry*. Columbia, Missouri:
University of Missouri Press, 1970.
Parkinson, Thomas, ed., *Robert Lowell: A Collection of Critical
Essays*. Englewood Cliffs, N.J.: Prentice-Hall, 1968.
Vendler, Helen, *Part of Nature, Part of Us*. Cambridge:
Harvard University Press, 1980.
Williamson, Alan, *Pity the Monsters: The Political Vision of
Robert Lowell*. New Haven: Yale University Press, 1974.

Yenser, Stephen, *Circle to Circle*. Berkeley: University of California Press, 1974.

ESSAYS

Since Yenser, pp. 354–57, has a very full listing up to 1973, I list here only items missing from Yenser's list, or items published after its appearance.

Fein, Richard J., "The Life of *Life Studies*," *The Literary Review* XXIII (1980): 326–38.

Hagopian, John V., "Robert Lowell's *Skunk Hour*," *Insight III: Analyses of English and American Poetry*, Reinhold Schiffer and Herman J. Weiand eds., Frankfurt: Hirschgraben Verlag, 1969.

Raffel, Burton, "Robert Lowell's *Life Studies*," *The Literary Review* XXIII (1980): 293–325.

————, "Robert Lowell's *Imitations*," *Translation Review* #5 (Summer, 1980): 20–27.

Index

MODERN LITERATURE SERIES

In the same series (continued from page ii)